Peacock Publishing & Alchemy
Workbook Series

Herbal Alchemy:
A Practical Manual of
Spagyrics

An illustrated guide to making
herbal medicines

By Frater M.T.O

Frist Edition

First Printing, 2017

Library of Congress Cataloging-in-Publication Data

ISBN-13: 978-1-944963-00-2

Peacock Publishing
A Subsidiary of Aretz, LLC
9635 W Colfax Ave.
Lakewood, CO 80215, USA
www.peacockpublishing.net

DEDICATION

To the group of students who took the first rounds of my in person Alchemy class, from which this book is directly drawn. You each started this journey along with me, and for that I thank you. Some of you I still have connections with, some of you have moved on, but each of you influenced me as an alchemist, magician, teacher, and friend. I dedicate this book to each of you: Julie, Bria, Crystal, Monticue, Amy, Marla, Cynthia, Sandra, Charlotte, Patrick, Colen, Nina, David, Becky and Ron.

And a special dedication to my late daughter, Bria, I still have the Lavender tincture that you made in that first round of classes. It is infused with your energy and spirit, and it is one of my most treasured possessions. It uplifts me up and brings a bit of your love when I need it most. I have some small bit of your Sulphur and Mercury within the Salts of your tincture, and I love you now and forever.

ACKNOWLEDGMENTS

I would like to give thanks to quite a few people who have assisted me with this book. Many of these are the same as my first book, but these two were originally one text, which was broken up due to color printing constraints.

To my Alchemical Teachers over the past two decades, who taught me, pushed me and encouraged me to make alchemy a truly personal journey.

To all of my students over the years, who have each taught me something valuable. Whether you taught me about yourself, herbs, alchemy, magic or myself when taking my classes. I grew as a person from watching you learn and grow, and we are both the better for it.

To Soror MIMM and Soror IA for proofing and trying to decipher my ramblings masquerading as writing.

Finally, to all of my children, Bria, Sena, Aidan, Lleyton and Molly. You are each my very own little Alchemical experiments; you have taught me so much in this laboratory of life, you are my true stones, my elixirs of life, my magnum opus, and I love you!

TABLE OF CONTENTS

INTRODUCTION: ABOUT THE ALCHEMY WORKBOOK SERIES AND THIS BOOK

About the Peacock Publishing Workbook series

The Peacock Publishing Workbook Series are meant to be just that, instructional books with valuable information for use as personal working journals, grimoires and chronicles of your own journey. Whether the topic is Alchemy, Magic, Herbalism, Tarot or other areas of study, the goal is to present a simple, concise, and easy-to-follow instructional guidebook for the aspirant to follow, free of unnecessary or over-complicated information.

In addition to the basic knowledge and material needed for each topic, each workbook presents a step-by-step procedure for practical applications, often accompanied by detailed pictures and photographs, to aid the aspirant in their work and performance of the process.

The Peacock Publishing Workbook Series includes guidance for personal journeys in Alchemy, Ceremonial Magic, Traditional Witchcraft, Herbalism, Freemasonry, Tarot and Egyptian Magic.

About this book

This book is a practical workbook on Herbal Alchemy, and covers the process of creating an herbal alchemical/spagyric tincture. Throughout this book, and the work that accompanies it, are references to the various Phases, Processes and Principles of Alchemy. These elements of Alchemy are covered in detail in the companion book, "Alchemical Theory: Unlocking the Mysteries of Alchemy, which is meant to accompany all of the Peacock Publishing workbooks on Alchemy. If you do not have that book yet, it is HIGHLY recommended that you obtain it, and work through it prior to undertaking any of the other workbooks in the series. It is critical to the understanding of the theories behind Alchemy that are used throughout all of these workbooks.

That being said, there are numerous books on "The Royal Art" known as alchemy available on the market, so what makes this one different? If you're like many who have been trying to find good, instructional books and materials on alchemy, you may have noticed that many books about alchemy are couched in archaic terms, symbols, acronyms, processes and procedures. So much so that attempting to follow or re-create the experiments and laboratory work given within them can prove extremely difficult for the beginner, if not near impossible. Even experienced alchemists will sometimes be confused or somewhat befuddled by material that often takes itself too seriously and makes things more complex than necessary.

The goal with this series of alchemy workbooks, is to create a simple, concise and easy to follow set of instructions for the alchemist to follow. In the first section, basic information is presented in an easy-to-understand fashion, and explains many of the archaic and symbolic procedures depicted in ancient alchemy texts to help lay the foundation for the second section, the practical part of the workbook. In the practical portion some additional information is given to explain specific phases, processes and principles that relate to the practical work. Precise step by step instructions are given, along with accompanying pictures and other directions pertaining to the work at hand. This is meant to guide the aspiring alchemist through the processes and its practical application without the need for additional resources. All efforts have been made to provide a list of supplies and equipment that are easy and inexpensive to obtain, if you do not already have many of them. In most cases, several examples of equipment will be given, including many items which are commonly found in most households.

Likewise, the spiritual exercises which accompany the practical work are designed to be easily performed by almost anyone. All that is needed is a quiet spot for meditation and contemplation for the duration of the exercises needed. No special attire, tools or accoutrements are required.

Many people do not understand that alchemy is not a physical process, nor is it a mental one or a spiritual one. Rather, it is a combination and a synthesis of all three. alchemy is composed of physical, mental and spiritual processes which, when combined, can have drastic effects upon one's existence, outlook and reality. The processes outlined in this (and other) workbooks are designed to be a type of self-initiation into the divine science of alchemy. The changes which occur within the alchemy student have been witnessed firsthand by the author after years of teaching this same material in an instructional classroom format.

How to use this book

This book is designed to be used as a true workbook. The instructions are step by step, and will lead you through the entire process of creating an Alchemical Herbal Tincture. It is not meant to skip around or peruse, unless you are already familiar with this process. Obviously, it may help to read through the entire book once, and then go back and follow the instructions step by step. However, the physical, mental and spiritual exercises found in the Practical section are designed to be done in order and for the length of time specified (generally one to two weeks per exercise). This gives the exercises and meditations time to be assimilated into your psyche, your mind, your spirit, your aura and thus allows it to have a permanent and lasting effect upon you. This aspect will be discussed in more depth later in this book.

The Alchemy Workbook Series of Books

The following books are available now or planned publications within the Alchemy Workbook series:

Alchemical Theory: Unlocking the Mysteries of Alchemy
Herbal Alchemy: A Practical Manual of Spagyrics
Herbal Alchemy: Spagyric Medicines
Herbal Alchemy: Creating the 7 Planetary Stones
Mineral Alchemy: Making an Alchemical Stone Elixir
Mineral Alchemy: Constructing an Artificial Stone
Magical Alchemy: Working with Herbal Spirits

Magical Alchemy: Ritual Alchemy of the Golden Dawn
Masonic Alchemy: The Sprig of Acacia

An updated list of currently available as well as planned titles can be found at the website: peacockpublishing.net/current-publications and peacockpublishing.net/upcoming-publications respectively.

CHAPTER 1: INTRODUCTION TO HERBAL ALCHEMY

The term Herbal Alchemy is used to describe alchemical operations, which were traditionally performed on minerals or metals, being enacted upon herbal or plant material. The terms 'herbal alchemy' and 'spagyrics' are often used interchangeably in many works, although some would consider Spagyrics to be a sub-category of herbal alchemy. When looking at some of the ways in which you can work with plants and herbs in alchemy you can extract herbal tinctures; create the Primum Ens; create plant stones; and working with the spirit of the plants and herbs for spiritual growth. This last item has some crossover with what we call 'Magical Alchemy', and it has been categorized under that heading for this book.

Plants, just like minerals and metals, have their planetary correspondences, which helps to identify the physical and spiritual effectiveness of each individual herb. Plants, by their nature, are very easy and mostly forgiving to work with. If one is interested in pursuing a deeper understanding of alchemy, studying the alchemical work enacted upon plants can be an excellent place to start. Mineral, and particularly Metallic alchemy, often use caustic and dangerous chemicals. Indeed, a well-known alchemist, Israel Regardie, burned his lungs when fumes of Antimony escaped in his lab work and he breathed in the fumes. Afterwards, he gave his alchemy lab equipment to a friend, but for the rest of his life, he suffered from the effects of the accident, and used an oxygen tank often later in his life. This should be a warning not to avoid alchemy, but rather to practice with the utmost care and safety.

Within the realm of herbal alchemy, there are several sub-sets of alchemical work, including Tinctures/Spagyrics, The Primum Ens and Plant/Vegetable Stones.

Tinctures/Spagyrics

A tincture, sometimes also called a Spagyric is an herbal mixture, typically a medicine in the form of a tincture, elixir or tonic, produced by alchemical means and processes. These procedures often involve the processes of conjunction, dissolution, separation, calcination, and the extraction and transformation of specific components from the ash of the plant. All the constituents of the plant are utilized, not just the oils.

In short, Spagyrics is the use of the alchemical stages, processes and principles specifically enacted upon plant matter and material. Often this use of Spagyrics is for healing purposes, whether healing of body, mind or spirit, and it is the forerunner to many modern medicines. Thus, a Spagyric is a holistic form of natural medicine which treats the whole of the individual—body, mind and spirit.

Our modern pharmaceuticals are nothing but scientific creations based upon the elixirs, tinctures and potions of the alchemist, the medicine man, the witch doctor and the local village madman. In fact, in 2015 it was discovered that a 1,000-year-old recipe for an herbal treatment found in a book called "Bald's Leechbook", was more effective than modern antibiotics when fighting a specific type of staph infection[1]. The experiment was carried out using the scientific method, and was validated at multiple universities. The ancient alchemists and herbalists certainly understood the medicines with which they worked, and were well aware of their capabilities.

Modern aspirin (or acetylsalicylic acid) dates to ancient Egypt. Hippocrates referred to the use of a salicylic tea to reduce fevers around 400BCE. Modern medicine now artificially manufactures this natural pain reliever, but where did our ancient predecessors find it? In the bark of the White Willow tree.   Thus, the modern-day alchemist may create a tincture of Willow Bark, which when completed as an alchemical tincture, not only has the physical benefits of pain relief, but is so much more potent due to its accompanying effects upon the mind and spirit as well. It is also the belief of most alchemists that a natural cure is of course more beneficial and more easily absorbed and used by the body than a synthetic substance.

Today's modern pharmaceuticals are targeted to very specific symptoms and causes. These medicines are much more specific and of a stronger nature than our natural immune systems and how our bodies are accustomed to being treated naturally. Hence, while their nature of being so specific is somewhat like a surgical scalpel in its base nature, it's strength and efficacy is more like using a jackhammer on our bodies and immune systems. Often, our body only needs a nudge in the right direction to allow it's natural healing mechanisms to kick in. Herbal medicines are more holistic in nature, and give the body that needed 'nudge' in the right direction. This is easier on the body, more natural and for those interested in a holistic sense of health, makes much more sense.

For example, if one has high cholesterol, there are a multitude of pharmaceuticals that can be taken. These are very specifically targeted

---

[1] http://www.bbc.com/news/uk-england-nottinghamshire-32117815

to reduce cholesterol found within the blood system. However, they also introduce numerous side effects, such as muscle pain and soreness, inflammation, liver and kidney damage and more. These medications are so powerful, they are like hitting the body with a sledgehammer to have the simple effect of lowering cholesterol. Using an herbal tonic, made up for example of Garlic, Turmeric, Skullcap and Ginger (all herbs believed to help in lowering cholesterol within the blood system), is a more natural and moderate way to reduce cholesterol. There are few side effects and it can be just as powerful in lowering cholesterol as pharmaceutical medicines. This has a gentler effect upon the body, that does not assault the bodily systems like a sledgehammer, but rather is more like using scalpel and forceps, certainly a much gentler way. That being said, before discontinuing the use of any prescription medications in favor of an herbal treatment, you should always consult with your physician as well as an herbalist in coming up with a plan to monitor your progress during the transition period. Never stop medications given to you by a medical professional until you have a chance to discuss the details with them.

Often, alchemy consisted of utilizing metallic substances, such as lead or mercury. Many of the chemicals used for various processes of transmutation of such metals, can be caustic and dangerous. In our modern world, Spagyrics is one method of working within the confines of the alchemical process, enabling the alchemist to be able to perform practical alchemy, both external and internal, exoteric and esoteric, in a much safer environment and on substances that are not dangerous to living things. Many alchemists begin working with Spagyrics and graduate to mineral/metallic alchemy after gaining a certain level of experience.

With Spagyrics, care must still be taken, as some herbs and plant materials can be harmful, some even deadly, but the processes themselves are relatively safe. One example of a resultant Spagyric formulation is typically called a tincture, and it has a transformative effect upon the alchemist, not only through the process of its creation, but also through its use as an herbal remedy, to heal mind, body and spirit.

The Primum Ens

The Primum Ens is seen as one of the most powerful rejuvenating medicines of the Plant Kingdom, and therefore is classified under Herbal Alchemy. The 'Primum Ens' is considered to be a thing in its first beginning, its first entity or Prima Materia; an invisible and intangible spiritual substance, which may be incorporated in some material vehicle. The Primum Ens is a type of tincture made with tartar oil as the first solvent, and then later with the spirit of wine. An herbal tincture, or Spagyric, begins with all 3 Principles, the Salt, Sulphur and Mercury, whereas the Ens does not, only the Sulphur and Mercury are present (sometimes referred to as a 'vulgar tincture'). Like tinctures and other scientific arena, there are multiple ways and different processes for creating the Primum Ens. In some of these, the outcome can certainly be somewhat different, but that makes them no less valid.

Plant/Vegetable Stones

In the world of alchemy, the Alchemical Stone is the most sought-after accomplishment. There are different types of stones, as well as different uses and attributions to each stone. There are artificial stones, in which a neutral 'Salt' substance is infused with the herbal oils and attributes of a plant. These often will have a use such as mental, magical or something more from the unseen world. These are a great way to familiarize oneself with the process of creating a stone, and they have benefits and uses in their own right. Next, there are plant stones, which also contain specific energies, such as creating an elemental or a planetary stone. Additionally, plant stones are often used in healing, both energetic for the mind and spirit, as well as physical healing and regenerative effects upon the body. The plant stones could be thought of as an extremely concentrated and potent tincture, in a solid form. Creating the artificial and plant stones have amazing effects upon the body, mind and spirit of the alchemist, and represent a certain level of adepthood within herbal alchemy. While an alchemist is never 'finished' with his alchemy (until and unless he completes the Magnum Opus and walks off into immortality), completing the creation of a certain number of plant stones represents a graduation of sorts, and certainly signifies a high level of accomplishment.

Working with plants within Alchemy can be a lifelong pursuit. It also offers the opportunity to work within the Alchemical processes in a safer environment and using materials that are less volatile than when typically working with minerals or metals. Once mastered, the process can be repeated and continued, as the number of herbs available for use are practically infinite.

This book focuses on the creation of an herbal alchemical or spagyric tincture. It will take you step by step through the entire process, and is accompanied by numerous pictures, detailing each step of the process so that you can follow along with ease. This process is designed to be undertaken over a period of 10 weeks. While it is possible, especially with experience, to do them in a shorter amount of time. However, it is highly recommended that you follow each step in the allotted time given, if not a bit longer. It is critical to take the recommended time in order to allow the inner work enough time to process, penetrate and affect the desired change.

That being said, it's time to get to work. Time to move on to the alchemical work!

CHAPTER 2 – WEEK 1 PREPARATION FOR ALCHEMICAL/SPAGYRIC WORK

Week 1 Alchemical Procedures - Introduction

As stated previously, alchemy is not a physical process, nor a mental one, nor a spiritual one, but rather it is a synthesis of all three. This means that while some small benefit may be gained solely by doing the physical work listed here, or that while some internal changes may be seen by simply performing the meditations found here, or that some progress might be made simply by reading and assimilating the information, the whole of all of these worked together is MUCH greater than the sum of its parts.

As you connect physically, spiritually and energetically with an herb of your choosing, the changes enacted upon it in conjunction with the meditations performed will likely far exceed your expectations for change within yourself. Alchemy is a life-changing process, and one that is not just experienced once, but many times over! The process repeats itself again and again, as we continue to purify and enlighten ourselves, raising ourselves to a higher state of spiritual evolution, and becoming 'more' than human. It is of critical importance to read all the information in the first section of this book, and complete both the physical experiments and the processes listed here in conjunction with the meditations and internal work. Lastly it is extremely important to journal your work. Having a baseline to reflect upon later, as well as being able to see changes taking place within yourself is a critical component to alchemical, and really any form of spiritual work.

Week 1 Alchemical Laboratory Work – Gathering Needed Materials

There are several things that you will need for your practical alchemical work. Many are household items, and nearly all of them can be procured at a home supply or hardware store. You should start gathering the items this week to begin to prepare for the upcoming alchemical lab work.

- The Dried Herb of your choice (Lemon Balm is highly recommended, if you don't already have something else in mind or are having trouble deciding what herb to use)
- Mortar and Pestle
- Clear Brandy for the Menstruum
- 2 Canning Jars with lids
- Wax Paper
- Aluminum Foil
- Cheesecloth
- Pyrex/Corning ware Heat Resistant Baking Dish
- Glass or wooden stirring sticks (coffee stirrers or kabob skewers can work well for this)
- Tupperware or another glass container to store your herb
- Propane Torch
- Stainless Steel Bowl
- Kitchen Sieve
- Distilled Water
- Razor Blades

If you are unsure of some of these items, you will see examples of them found in the pictures that follow. These items can typically be obtained for around (or less than) fifty dollars. For everyday items, such as the baking dish, canning jars and stainless steel bowl, as a beginner in alchemy, if you already have one used for cooking, feel free to use it to begin this process. Just ensure that it is washed and cleaned very well prior to alchemical use. If you intend on pursuing alchemy long-term, and plan on making many more tinctures in the future, then it is highly recommended that you purchase one solely for use when making alchemical tinctures, rather than one that is shared for mundane use. Please note that the process of calcination WILL scorch and put burn marks on the stainless-steel bowl, and it will likely not be suitable for cooking or other purposes afterwards. Or at the very least, it won't look very pretty.

Week 1 Alchemical Meditational Work – Entering the Alchemy Lab

A Note on Meditation

Options are given in this workbook to accommodate a range of experiences in meditations. These options vary between 5 and 20 minutes in length. If you are experienced at meditation, then 20 minutes is likely not going to be a huge challenge. Given a purpose, and a substance on which to focus, 20 minutes can fly by for those with experience at meditation. However, if you are new to a meditational practice, 20 minutes can not only seem like a lifetime, but it would probably be a waste of your time. If you are a beginner to meditation, that's GREAT! There are no problems if you are new to meditation, simply follow the instructions here and jump right in! It is a very useful skill, and one that you will improve upon just while working through this workbook. Trying to bench press 500 lbs. on your first day at the gym is not only setting you up for failure, it would likely cause physical damage as well. While there is no danger here in these basic meditations, trying to meditate for 10, 15 or 20 minutes when you are new to meditation is only setting you up for failure. Set a time that you feel you could accomplish (probably not less than 5 minutes though), and work on it. You'll find it becomes easier and easier as you practice. It may help, especially at first, to use some type of voice recorder (many cell phones have a recording function) to record the meditations, and use that to walk yourself through them. The point is not to worry too much about whether you've spent enough time, but focusing and spending quality time in meditation no matter how experienced you might be.

Week 1 Alchemical Meditation - Entering the Alchemy Lab

Meditation is not only a useful skill and practice to have, but it is healthy for the mind, body and spirit. During meditation, there are opportunities for us to learn and grow in many ways. Some of the goals in this type of meditation are purification, reconnection, restoration, and circulation of the life force throughout the vessel, the vessel in this case, being you. In other words, just as you might pour two different solutions into a jar, and then swirl them around to mix them, so it is with meditation. We are swirling around the energies, purifications, calcinations and other processes and practices, to enact and cause change within ourselves.

You should use this "Entering the Alchemy Lab" meditation (or some form thereof) any time before beginning your alchemical work. It is also advisable to use this meditation just prior to your weekly meditations, flowing directly out of this one and into your weekly meditation.

Reaching a true state of relaxation can be very difficult, especially for the beginner. In today's world, we are often so caught up in the hectic and rushed nature of everyday life, that it can be difficult for us to slow down and just have some quiet time to ourselves. This meditation of "Entering the Alchemy Lab" is one of progressive relaxation, and it may take you a few times to learn to achieve and maintain a relaxed state. It allows you to focus only on your breathing, and on one part of your body at a time. Its simple nature makes it easy to use, and it has great effects in preparing the mind, body and spirit for deeper states of meditation and contemplation.

If you wish to visualize your own personal alchemy lab, complete with beakers, vessels, ovens, distillation apparatus and more, feel free to do so. However, such in-depth visualization skills and astral creation work are a bit beyond the scope of this book. However, instructions on doing so will be coming out in a future workbook.

Entering the Alchemy Lab

1. Begin by closing your eyes and becoming aware of your breathing. Take a deep breath in through the nose; allow your stomach to expand as you breathe in. Hold the breath for a few seconds and then breathe out your mouth slowly, allowing your body to completely relax on the out breath.
2. Take note of sounds that you may hear. It may be cars driving by, the shifting of your chair, children playing in another room, or dogs barking. Know that these sounds are around you, but they do not interfere with your meditative state.
3. Also, take note of the feelings about you. The chair on which you are sitting or the floor on which you are lying. The touch of your clothes upon your body, any breeze that may be passing by, touching you and leaving a sensation in its wake. Know that these feelings are around you, but that they also do not interfere with your meditative state.
4. Consciously slow your breathing down with each breath you take. Breathe in through your nose; hold it for a few seconds, and then exhale out your mouth and again hold for a few seconds. With each breath, you take your body is becoming more relaxed and your mind is becoming more clear and focused. Breathing in through your nose, holding it for a few seconds, and then exhaling out your mouth and holding for a few seconds. Your breathing is becoming measured, deep and rhythmic.
5. Now with each breath, visualize a stream of white light travelling into the crown of your head. This energy travels down and throughout your entire body, and fills your body with this pure white light.

6. Breathe in the light through your nose and bring your awareness to your face. Allow any tension in your forehead, your eyes, and jaw to relax as you breathe out. Your face is now completely relaxed.

7. Again, breathe in the light through your nose and bring your awareness to your throat, neck and shoulders. As you breathe in, focus on any tension in your neck and throat and particularly your shoulders to release with the out breath.

8. Again, breathe in the light through your nose and see it travelling down each of your arms, all the way to your fingertips. Feel your arms dropping, as they relax, being filled with this light, and any tightness or tension is dissipated as you exhale.

9. Again, breathe in the light; and as you do you see the light travelling around your chest and heart area. As the light swirls around your heart area, you feel a sense of warmth, comfort and love. Exhale deeply, allowing any tensions in your chest to dissolve and leave with the exhaled breath.

10. Again, breathe in the light and bring your awareness to your stomach. Allow your stomach to expand completely with light. As you breathe out, release any tension found in your stomach area.

11. Take a deep breath in through your nose, and as you do, see the light coming in and travelling down your spine. Your spine is filling with light, releasing any tension in the discs and joints as you breathe out.

12. Breathe in the Light and bring your awareness to your hips, dissolving any tension there, and as you exhale allow your hips to relax.

13. Again, breathe in the light and see the light travelling into your upper legs and thighs, releasing all tension and stress on the out breath. Any tension in your thighs is being released now.

14. Again, breathe in the light and bring your awareness to your lower legs. You see white light travelling into your knees and lower legs and releasing all tension and stiffness. Any tension in your calves is being released now as you exhale.

15. As you breathe in the Light again, bring your awareness to your feet. See the Light permeating your feet, from the instep to the sole, from the heels to the tips of your toes. Exhale and see and feel any tension in your feet being released on the out breath.

16. Now once again breathe in this Light and allow this beautiful light to go to any parts of your body that need healing. It could be a past injury or simply a weakness in your body that you are aware of. Simply allow the light to completely surround this part of your body now. Your entire body is now full of this beautiful white light.

17. And now the light expands into your aura. It expands beyond the physical boundaries of your body and permeates the energy field in your aura. See this light releasing any energy in your aura that needs to be released, that is not supporting you, filling in any cracks or holes that may be present. See your physical body, your energy centers and your aura glowing with this divine healing energy. See your aura like an egg; very strong and free from holes and imbalances.

18. Your body is feeling very relaxed now. Your mind is clear and focused. Your emotions are feeling calm and content. Rest here a few moments…See yourself in your mind's eye entering your own personal alchemy lab. Walking through the door into your practical lab, ready to begin the work ahead.

19. It is now time to leave this meditation and move on. When you feel ready, gently bring your awareness back to your body, and to the room you are in. Hear once again the sounds around you, the feeling of the chair under you as you return to full consciousness. Give your fingers and toes a wiggle and gently open your eyes – coming back to waking consciousness.

Week 1 Alchemical Homework

During the first week, you should begin to gather all the materials together that you will need for the remainder of the tincture process. Additionally, you should begin performing the "Entering the Alchemy Lab" meditation at least 3 times during the week. Upon completing each meditation, you should journal any feelings, experiences or insights that you had during meditation. Don't worry if your mind wandered occasionally or if you got off track. The important thing is to keep working at it and bring your focus back when your mind does wander. You are setting up a practice of meditation and journaling, which will lay the groundwork for the rest of the alchemical work that lay ahead.

Week 1 Summary

This first week is a week of preparation. You will be preparing for physical/laboratory alchemical work by beginning to gather the necessary components for the physical work. You will be preparing for the meditational and spiritual alchemical work by beginning to work the first mediation, "Entering the Alchemy Lab". This mediation should not only be practiced this week, but should preface all your meditations throughout the course of the exercises in this book. Whatever you do, do not look at this week as a wasted one. Even if you already have EVERYTHING you need, and you are experienced or adept at meditation, take this week to set the stage for next week's work. If you have everything you need then organize it and lay it out. If you don't have a dedicated alchemy space then find a box or storage container in which to keep it neat and organized. Practice the meditation to prepare for the further steps that will be coming as we move forward in this book. While it is a week for preparation, it is not a week of laziness, the work begins now!

Alchemical Journal
A Note on Journaling

Journaling is a critical component of any type of magical, meditational or self-developmental work. It allows us to see where we've been, keeps details of lessons learned, insights gleaned and personal growth achieved. They can be short and sweet, long and wordy or anywhere in between. The important thing is that you write down SOMETHING about the experience that you just had. You should journal immediately after any work or experience, and it is also wise to leave at least a few lines to add a comment later regarding the experience, as oftentimes insights and additional knowledge or information will come our way after the fact.

For example, in working with your herb, perhaps in your meditation you will see a symbol. You should journal that symbol and describe as well as draw it. A few days or weeks later, perhaps you see that symbol and then you will understand WHY you had been shown it during your meditation. Leaving a few lines to add to your entry about the experience of seeing the symbol a few days later may be critical to reading and fully understanding that experience 3-4 years down the road.

When journaling, there are various patterns that you will come to notice over time. Some of those involve astrological timing, signs and their relationship to your own astrological natal chart. As such, in the journaling pages that follow are included places to record some basic information regarding the date, time, sun sign, moon sign and moon phase during the time when you performed the meditation. This information can come in handy down the road, when you begin comparing your varied and multiple alchemical works to one another. It is always interesting to find that you have the most insights during a waxing moon, or that your work is especially powerful when the Sun in is Aries. Following that information, are lined pages for you to journal your actual experiences.

Week 1 Alchemical Journal - Entry 1

Name: _____ Date/Time: _____

Sun Sign: _____ Moon Sign: _____

Moon Phase: New / Waxing / Full / Waning / VoC

_____
_____
_____
_____
_____
_____
_____
_____
_____
_____
_____
_____
_____
_____
_____
_____
_____
_____
_____
_____
_____
_____
_____

Week 1 Alchemical Journal - Entry 2

Name: _____ Date/Time: _____

Sun Sign: _____ Moon Sign: _____

Moon Phase: New / Waxing / Full / Waning / VoC

_____

_____

_____

_____

_____

_____

_____

_____

_____

_____

_____

_____

_____

_____

_____

_____

_____

_____

_____

_____

_____

_____

_____

_____

_____

_____

Week 1 Alchemical Journal - Entry 3

Name: _____ Date/Time: _____

Sun Sign: _____ Moon Sign: _____

Moon Phase: New / Waxing / Full / Waning / VoC

_____

_____

_____

_____

_____

_____

_____

_____

_____

_____

_____

_____

_____

_____

_____

_____

_____

_____

_____

_____

_____

_____

_____

_____

_____

_____

CHAPTER 3 – WEEK 2 CHOOSING YOUR HERB

Week 2 Alchemical Procedures

By now, you may be asking yourself what herb you would like to use to create your tincture. This is a very personal decision, but you may choose any herb that is safe to ingest. If you are unsure as to the potential dangers of a given herb, you should visit a local apothecary, or contact an herbalist (in person or online) to discuss the herb of your choice. At our apothecary, our local herbalist (who wrote the introduction to this book) is available for local or remote consultations. You can visit her website at www.gypsyherbalist.com if you are interested in discussing your chosen herb with a qualified herbalist.

There are many areas and associations that you may use to choose your herb. Some of these areas are:

- Associations to the Elements
- Associations to the Zodiac
- Associations to the Planets

- Associations to the Kabbalah
- Associations within your tradition
- An Herb chosen for a specific healing purpose
- A favorite Herb that has always spoken to you and has personal meaning

Here are a few examples of Herbs and some of their attributions (these are examples using one set of associations, which may vary from tradition to tradition):

Example 1

Mugwort is related to the Element of Water, and to the Zodiacal sign of Cancer and to the planet Venus. If I wanted to overcome an emotional incident, I might choose Mugwort because it is related to Water. If I was a Cancer Sun sign, or wished to enhance that aspect of my nature, I might choose Mugwort. Likewise, if I wanted to improve my relationship with my spouse or significant other, I might choose Mugwort because of its relationship to Venus.

Example 2

Dandelion is related to the Element of Air, and to the Zodiacal sign of Libra and to the planet Neptune. Perhaps I am undergoing an educational pursuit, going back to school or other form of study, I might choose Dandelion as the Element of Air is associated to the mind and the learning process. If I were a Libra, or wished to enhance that aspect of my nature, I might choose Dandelion. Perhaps I wish to improve my spirituality or mystical pursuits, I might choose Dandelion because of its association to Neptune.

Example 3

If I were involved in a tradition that used Acacia as a centerpiece of the tradition (such as Freemasonry), I might choose to make a tincture of one of those, to enhance my connection with and knowledge of my tradition. This tincture could be used prior to engaging in meditative or ritual activities to enhance the connection to the energy of that current.

Example 4

Perhaps you were born under a Fire sign, and have very little or no Earth in your chart. You may choose to make a tincture from an herb associated to Earth to improve and enhance that aspect of your nature and improve on a weak area of your personality.

Dried vs. Fresh Herbs

One of the questions that many people ask is, should I use dried herbs or fresh herbs? Working with both is a good experience, however it is advisable to begin working with dried herbs. The Sulphur, or oils, are still contained within the dried herb, and being able to see those oils drawn out is an alchemical process all on its own. Also, using fresh herbs can introduce unwanted water and other parts of the plant that may be less desirable to have in your completed tincture. There are also specific methods of alchemy and spagyrics that use fresh herbs, but for the preparations that we are using, a dried herb works best.

You should try to obtain your herb from an apothecary with a good reputation. Many metaphysical shop's carry various herbs, and there are also health and organic food stores that may carry dried herbs. Many herbs can also be found online as well. If you do not know where to obtain your herb, you can obtain them at a quality online outlet, such as Ye Olde Magic Shoppe, Home of the Herbalist and the Alchemist Apothecary (store.yeoldemagicshoppe.com).

Choosing your Herb

Now that you have a few ideas of how to choose different types of herbs, it's time to decide which herb you will use to make an alchemical tincture. It would be beneficial to be able to choose an herb that not only appeals to you, but represents an area of your life that you would like to work on. This will allow you to connect with your herb, and provide you with a purpose and goal that will give you a specific path to move forward. If you are unsure, or don't have an immediate area of your life or person that you would like to work on, a good generic herb to use, is Lemon Balm (botanical name: Melissa Officinalis). It is forgiving to work with for the beginner, and has numerous health and spiritual benefits.

The Herb that I have chosen to use is:

_____

(Go ahead, write it in there, don't feel bad…this is a Workbook after all! You'll be writing in this book a lot in the upcoming chapters!)

Week 2 Alchemical Laboratory Work

The laboratory work this week is limited. You should obtain your herb, and get to know it. Physically, what does the herb look like? How does it feel to the touch? What does it smell like? Is it woody, leafy or a root? Does it have flowers? If you crush a small bit between your fingers, does the smell change? This week is all about investigation. The better you know your herb now, the easier it will be to connect with your herb as you begin to transform it over the upcoming weeks. Make note of these things, and don't limit yourself to a single sitting. Be present with your herb multiple times this week, get to know it and become fast friends! You may want to begin to give energy and purpose to your herb at this point. Infusing your herb with energy and purpose is a huge part of the alchemical tincture process. You will give energy to your herb and other materials throughout the entire process. In the end, your tincture will be more powerful, effective and potent due to the energy that you have given it. In return, your tincture will then give back to you that energy exponentially, in the form of healing and purpose.

A Note on Projecting Energy

There are numerous ways to project and send energy to something, whether it be a living entity or inanimate object. There are some very specific means which are used within various traditions and practices as well as more generic and general forms of energy transference. Within some traditions, the finger and eyes are important tools with which to transfer energy, while in others it may be the heart or throat chakra places upon the human body. Here you will find a few generic means by which you may experiment and use for sending energy into your herb and tincture substance. It is not required that you use these methods. If you have your own more specific method, by all means feel free to use those.

1. Cupping-Cupping consists of sitting down with your herb or tincture material held on your lap or between your legs. Cup your hands on either side of your material and envision your energy and purpose flowing from above and within yourself, out of your palms and into the material.

2. The Triangle-The Triangle method consists of sitting down with your herb or tincture material held on your lap or between your legs. Form a triangle with your thumbs and index fingers, and place this triangle just above your material. Envision energy flowing from above you, into your body and out of your heart center, through the triangle and into your material.

3. Fingers and Eyes-With this method, you will place your herb or tincture material on a table or desk in front of you. Extend the fingers of both hands and point them at the material. Envision energy coming from above you, filling your body with pure white light. Next, see this energy flowing both out of your fingers as well as out of your eyes and into your material, as you stare at it intently.

4. Body Alignment-If your tincture is for a specific healing purpose, place and hold your material at and on a specific part of your body, and envision energy flowing from yourself into the material. For example, if it is for love or a matter of the physical heart, hold it against your chest and heart and see energy transferring from yourself into the material. If it is for sexual reproduction or stimulation hold it against your loins and again see energy transferring from yourself into the material. If it is for digestive issues, hold it against your stomach and see energy transferring from yourself into the material. If it is to help you to open your 3rd Eye Chakra, hold the material against your forehead and again see energy transferring from yourself into the material.

5. Association-There are numerous other associations that you may use, including Elemental, Kabbalistic and the Chakra's. For example, if the tincture is of an earthly nature, you may place the tincture at your feet and see energy transferring from yourself to your tincture through your feet, your own contact with the Earth. If it is for Air, you could hold the tincture to your head, the place of intellect and again see the airy energy transferring from yourself and into your material. If it is for Fire, you could hold the material against the area of your loins, and if it were for Water, you could place it against your Heart area. Likewise, with both the Kabbalah and the Chakra's, you could place the tincture against your body at the place representing the associated Sephirah, path or Chakra, and see the energy transferring from that part of your body and into the material.

These are just a few methods of transferring energy. If you're new to energy work, don't worry, it's an easier process than you might think, and the visualization of the energy transfer is very important. Don't forget, regardless of the method used, you should not only send energy from yourself and the divine into your material, but you should infuse it with a specific purpose. This purpose is the one that you have decided upon, and is your reason for making this particular tincture or herbal medicine.

Figure 6.1-The Dried Herb or Materium

Figure 6.2-Placing the material in the vessel
(yes, in this case a simple mason jar is considered a 'vessel')

Week 2 Alchemical Meditational Work

Now that you have chosen your herb, over the upcoming week, you should perform at least 3 meditations with your herb. It is very beneficial to be able to hold your herb, or at least a portion of it, in your hands during meditation, so that you can better connect with it as you meditate. You may also choose to feel, smell or even taste it during your meditations. Depending on where you obtained your herb, it will likely be in some type of a zip lock baggie. If not, you may place it in one, or put it in one of your mason jars, so that it can be sealed, but also so that you can unseal it for your meditations, and can feel, smell and taste your herb.

Meditate on the reasons why you have chosen that particular herb; what do you hope to accomplish with your herb? Meditate on the associations of your herb. See in your mind the External qualities, the 'Salt' of your herb; the shape, texture, smell and feel of it. Now see the herb transforming into a final and perfected state, providing you with the healing and internal qualities that you desire to obtain through the course of this alchemical process. Each meditation should last between 5 and 20 minutes on these points.

For this first mediation, here is a sample of what you might do for this meditation. Go through the 'Entering the Alchemy Lab' meditation to establish your breathing and relaxation and entering your personal lab and workplace. Once you have completed that, now turn your focus towards your herb. Feel it's physical state, notice its texture. Inhale the scent of your herb and if you wish, taste a very small bit of it. See the light of your aura and notice that the herb or plant also has an aura about it. Now see a small ribbon of energy snaking out from your aura and touching the light surrounding the herb. See them beginning to vibrate and resonate together, as the colors come closer and closer together until they match. Focus again on the feel, smell and taste of the herb as you connect with its energy. Now focus on your purpose in choosing your herb and what it is that you hope to accomplish. Talk to the herb, communicate with it and request that the spirit of the herb help you in your search for the purpose, be it healing of body, mind or spirit. Thank the spirit of the herb for its presence and its assistance. After a moment, return your attention to your breathing making it slow and steady. Withdraw the ribbon of energy connecting you to your herb and when you are ready, return to yourself and open your eyes.

Next, use the journal pages that follow to record your feelings, thoughts and any experiences that you may have had during your meditation.

Week 2 Alchemical Homework

For this week, your homework is, 'get to know your herb'. That includes physically, becoming intimately familiar with what it looks like, smells like, tastes like. Also, you may want to do some research. Where does it typically grow? Does it thrive in dry and arid climates, or is it better in wet or cooler environments? Does it require a lot of water? How does it seed? Does it have berries? What are its natural health and healing benefits? What are its magical and spiritual attributes? Learn about your herb, get to know it, as you will become fast friends over the upcoming months. You should perform the meditational work 3 times this week, and each time should be between 5 and 20 minutes.

Week 2 Summary

Meet your new best friend! This week is all about learning about your herb, and beginning to form a relationship with it. This is truly the beginning of a beautiful friendship! Over the next few months, you will be giving of your time and energy to your herb, as you transform it (and yourself) through the alchemical phases and processes. As your herb changes, so will you change. This puts the two of you into an interesting and symbiotic relationship. Care for your herb as you would one of your children or best friends, going through a process of change. In return, at the end of the process, your herb will then give back to you of its energy, coupled with the energy and change which you have enacted upon it. The better you know your herb now, the easier it will be to connect and work with it over the upcoming weeks. Treat it as a good friend, and it will treat you even better in return.

Week 2 Alchemical Journal - Entry 1

Name: _____ Date/Time: _____

Sun Sign: _____ Moon Sign: _____

Moon Phase: New / Waxing / Full / Waning / VoC

_____

_____

_____

_____

_____

_____

_____

_____

_____

_____

_____

_____

_____

_____

_____

_____

_____

_____

_____

_____

_____

_____

_____

_____

_____

Week 2 Alchemical Journal - Entry 2

Name: _____ Date/Time: _____

Sun Sign: _____ Moon Sign: _____

Moon Phase: New / Waxing / Full / Waning / VoC

_____

_____

_____

_____

_____

_____

_____

_____

_____

_____

_____

_____

_____

_____

_____

_____

_____

_____

_____

_____

_____

_____

_____

Week 2 Alchemical Journal - Entry 3

Name: _____ Date/Time: _____

Sun Sign: _____ Moon Sign: _____

Moon Phase: New / Waxing / Full / Waning / VoC

_____

_____

_____

_____

_____

_____

_____

_____

_____

_____

_____

_____

_____

_____

_____

_____

_____

_____

_____

_____

_____

_____

_____

CHAPTER 4 – WEEK 3 PREPARING YOUR HERBAL SALTS AND THE MERCURY

Week 3 Alchemical Procedures - Preparing the Herb

For the next step in creating an alchemical tincture, you will be taking the herb that you have chosen, and grinding it into a coarse grind. This process is bringing forth and revealing the true Salt of the herb (remember, we are talking about the philosophical 'salt' of the herb, representing the physical nature and part of the plant, not table salt), and beginning to break down those Salts into a slightly different material. The herb needs to be broken down so that as it soaks in the Menstruum (or solution) for two weeks (beginning next week), the Sulphur (or essential oils in this case) of the herb will be released as much as possible. Do not grind your herb to a powder, you are merely breaking it down a bit, and you will be doing it 3 times, so make sure you don't over grind your herb. It is almost as much a symbolic process as a practical one, so don't grind it up too fine, keep it to a coarse grind.

You will also be preparing the Menstruum, or the Brandy in this case. Just as you prepared the Salts (which currently also contain the

Sulphur), you will want to prepare the Mercury, or the life-giving spirit. As the agent of change, it is just as important, if not more so at this point, to bless and energize the Menstruum solution before bringing the two together.

Week 3 Alchemical Laboratory Work - Preparing the Herb and the Menstruum

Week 3 Alchemical Lab Work - Preparing the Herb

First, you will again perform the meditation 'Entering the Alchemy Lab' to prepare for your alchemical work. Next, bless or energize your herb (or whatever process you or your tradition may choose to utilize). Give it energy, define your purpose, state your purpose in creating this herbal tincture aloud, say an invocation or blessing over it and send the energy and light of the divine universe into your material. This is a very important part of the entire alchemical process, as this sets the reason and intention of undertaking the practice in the first place. This separates your herb from the vulgar world, and sets it apart as a spiritual substance. It also solidifies the connection between yourself and your herb, so that the purpose that you have for this process, and the purpose you give the herb become united.

Next, as you grind your Herb, you should be in a semi-meditative state, with a focus on the purpose of your tincture. Keeping the herb in the Mortar and Pestle close to you, within your own Aura (much as you did when meditating with the herb), will allow you to keep in contact with your herb, both physically and energetically. See yourself releasing the Divine power of the herb as well as yourself, as you perform the work. Spend time with your herb, feel it, smell it, taste it, experience it, become it, as you do your work. Consider that this material will be your own alchemical child that you will conceive, create and nurture during the upcoming weeks, and you should treat it with love and respect.

It is important not to crush or grind it too fine or into a powder, as it will turn into a 'muddy' substance when the solution is added, and it will not drain or separate properly. You also want to avoid contact with any metals at this point in the procedure to avoid potentially unwanted chemical reactions.

After you have completed grinding your herb to the appropriate consistency, you should place it within the vessel and seal it.

Figure 7.1 and 7.2-The Materium in the Mortar and Pestle, prior to a coarse grind

Figure 7.3-The Herb after a coarse grind

Figure 7.4 and 7.5-Using a funnel to place the Materium in the vessel.
Figure 7.6-The Materium in the vessel to be sealed.

Week 3 Alchemical Lab Work - Preparing the Menstruum

Next week, you will be combining the Salt, or body of your material, with the Mercury, or Breath of Life to create (or in this case, draw out) the Sulphur, or soul, of your material. You have already properly prepared the Salt of your material, and so you must just as importantly, prepare the Mercury. The alcohol is an agent of change, and while it does not perform the actual purpose associated with your alchemical tincture, it is a critical component necessary for the change.

As always, you should perform the meditation 'Entering the Alchemy Lab' to prepare for your alchemical work. You should energize the alcohol in a similar fashion to how you energized or blessed your herb. Give it energy, define your purpose, state it out loud, say an invocation or blessing over it and send the energy and light of the divine universe into the alcohol. Additionally, since it has already been harvested and prepared, you should thank the earth for providing the fruit of the vine and say a blessing over it and send the energy and light of the divine into the alcohol.

As you did with the herb, you should seal the Mercury in its vessel for the upcoming week. Sealing both in their respective vessel's again sets them apart from the world, and keeps them prepared for the work ahead.

Figure 7.7-The Agent of Change in the vessel to be sealed.

Week 3 Alchemical Meditational Work

Now that you have gotten to know your herb, your connection with it should be even stronger. Connect with your herb this week, as you did last week. See it's aura, it's vibrational level, and tune yours to match it. Keeping it within the space of your aura, become one with your herb, as if it were part of you. Now think of your purpose that you have chosen for your tincture. Convey that purpose to your herb, feed it the energy of your intent. Now see that purpose within yourself. Just as you broke your herb down by grinding it this week, break down that habit, purpose or trait about yourself that you wish to change. If it is for healing, see the malady that it is to treat being broken down. This is not a simple breakdown by dissolving or disappearing, that will come later. This is breaking down an old sidewalk with a jackhammer or a sledgehammer, type of breaking down. For new growth to occur, the old must be broken down into something with which you can work. Just as hard baked soil must be broken up into soft, malleable earth before planting a garden, so must the part of ourselves that we wish to change be broken down, so that we can build something new. You may wish to visualize either of the two situations listed, see yourself with a sledgehammer breaking down a sidewalk, with the sidewalk being that part of yourself that you wish to change; or see it as a piece of hard-baked clay soil, that you must break up and till to prepare for the new growth. When you have finished breaking it down completely, take a moment in your mind's eye, to reach down with your hands, and pick up the pieces. Allow them to flow through and fall from your hands, falling back to the ground. Know that that part of yourself that you desire to change, has been broken up, and the transformation has now begun in earnest.

Know that while these changes have begun, and certain things in life may start adjusting themselves to compensate, you are committed and dedicated to following this through to the end. For just a moment, at the end of the meditation, see the soil, sidewalk or whatever analogy you may choose to use, shimmer and quickly become the result that you are seeking. Catch a glimpse of that future, and then allow it to return to its broken and prepared state.

Week 3 Alchemical Homework

You should (as always) perform the 'Entering the Alchemy Lab' meditation prior to beginning your work each week. You should perform the practical work 3 times, including grinding the herb in a Mortar and Pestle, blessing or energizing your menstruum solution, followed by performing the meditational work. It would be ideal to perform the meditation with your herb still present in the mortar and pestle, so that you can easily see, feel, smell and (optionally) taste your herb.

As previously stated, you do not want to over-grind your herb. If you feel that it is being ground too much after one or two times, feel free to make the grinding process a symbolic one. It is the connection that you make with the herb that is extremely important in this process.

You should perform the meditational work 3 times during this week, after each time you grind your herb, and each meditation should last between 5 and 20 minutes.

Next, use the journal pages that follow to record your feelings, thoughts and any experiences that you may have had during your meditations.

Week 3 Summary

Let the Games begin! And so, we are now off and running with our first alchemical physical work! The process of grinding the herb is the phase of Nigredo, the breakdown, and while not in actuality but metaphorically, it fits in part into the process of Fermentation, even though it is not 'fermented', part of fermentation is Putrefaction, or the breakdown of the substance, which you are artificially performing by using a mortar and pestle.

If you have not done any sort of spiritual or alchemical work before, it's time to fasten your seatbelts! Spiritual work such as this, tends to cause real change within yourself, and by extension your world around you. Change can be uncomfortable and even painful, so don't be surprised if some things around you start to fall apart or break down. But, persevere, and remember that it takes patience and dedication to effect true change within yourself and your world!

Week 3 Alchemical Journal - Entry 1

Name: _____ Date/Time: _____

Sun Sign: _____ Moon Sign: _____

Moon Phase: New / Waxing / Full / Waning / VoC

_____

_____

_____

_____

_____

_____

_____

_____

_____

_____

_____

_____

_____

_____

_____

_____

_____

_____

_____

_____

_____

_____

_____

Week 3 Alchemical Journal - Entry 2

Name: _____ Date/Time: _____

Sun Sign: _____ Moon Sign: _____

Moon Phase: New / Waxing / Full / Waning / VoC

_____

_____

_____

_____

_____

_____

_____

_____

_____

_____

_____

_____

_____

_____

_____

_____

_____

_____

_____

_____

_____

_____

_____

_____

_____

Week 3 Alchemical Journal - Entry 3

Name: _____ Date/Time: _____

Sun Sign: _____ Moon Sign: _____

Moon Phase: New / Waxing / Full / Waning / VoC

_____

_____

_____

_____

_____

_____

_____

_____

_____

_____

_____

_____

_____

_____

_____

_____

_____

_____

_____

_____

_____

_____

_____

_____

_____

_____

_____

_____

CHAPTER 5 – WEEK 4 & 5 THE CONCEPTION OF THE ALCHEMICAL CHILD

Week 4-5 Alchemical Procedures

In alchemy, Conjunction is a combining of two or more materials into a new substance. In this case, we are referring specifically to your Herb and the Menstruum, or solution (the Brandy). Now it is time to perform the first Conjunction of your material. Consider these two separate items as being a type of sacrament or repast, with you acting as the priest or priestess. The herb is similar to the bread, while the alcohol is analogous to the wine. At this point, as you prepare to combine the Herb and the Alcohol, it is the moment of the formation of your own alchemical child. You should look at this moment as a conception, the meeting of the sperm and egg, or the Mercury and Salt/Sulphur, and once again, you should say a blessing or energize your ingredients during this process.

As you complete your initial Conjunction, you should continue to see, feel, smell[2] and connect with this new substance that you have created. Once the Conjunction is completed, again charge it with energy, purpose and blessings.

You will now need to allow the new child to gestate. To do so properly, you will need to macerate, or shake up, your mixture several times per day. This will allow the solution and the herb to thoroughly mix, and allow the menstruum to draw out as much of the Sulphur as possible.

Week 4-5 Alchemical Laboratory Work

This week, you will perform a Conjunction of your herb and the menstruum solution. As always, perform the 'Entering the Alchemy Lab' meditation before beginning. When you are ready, you should give one last bit of energy to each one individually. It may also help to connect to your herb as you have in previous meditations, seeing a tendril connecting your aura with the aura of the herb. This will be the last time that you bless or energize them as separate entities. When ready, place the vessel containing the herb onto a stable surface, such as a table. Place yourself into a semi-meditative state as you did when grinding the herb in a mortar and pestle. Staying close to the vessel, so that it is within your aura, slowly begin to pour the menstruum solution into the vessel containing the herb. Do so slowly, do not rush it, do not simply 'pour' it in, as if pouring a glass of something to drink. As the menstruum flows into the vessel, notice the herb, how it moves, how it reacts, how quickly it takes on the color and attributes of the herb, already leeching out some of the Sulphur from the Salt. See the conception of your alchemical child, growing and filling the vessel. The herb should take up about 1/3 of the jar, and you should pour in enough solution to fill the jar around

---

[2] When smelling your herb after the alcohol has been added, use your sense of smell in a long, steady intake of breath. This will allow your sense of smell to become used to the smell of the alcohol before smelling the herb. If you only take a short, fast breath, you will likely only smell alcohol.

2/3 full, leaving a bit of room at the top for the gasses and air to move and expand.

Over the next two weeks, you will need to Macerate your substance. In this case, the process of Maceration will consist of you shaking your substance once, or preferably twice per day. This will allow the Mercury (Brandy) to permeate through the entire substance of the Salt, to withdraw the most Sulphur from the herbal material. Throughout this process, you should continue to connect with your alchemical child each time you shake it up. You should spend time with it each day, continuing to energize it and give it purpose. Watch it change and grow, watch as the color and consistency deepen and thicken. Simply shaking it each day will macerate the substance, but will not infuse the mixture with the purpose for which you are performing this experiment, and the neglect of the internal alchemy will yield neglect of the external alchemy as well. You should avoid removing the lid often throughout the process and allowing the gasses created by the solution to escape. You may perhaps once or twice remove the lid to smell and connect with the substance, as well as to check the state of the Wax Paper covering. Limit this to once per week at most. When completed, you may wish to wrap your entire jar in aluminum foil in order to keep out any rays of light, which can potentially cause unwanted chemical reactions.

Figures 8.1, 8.2 and 8.3-Conception of the Alchemical Child by Conjunction, adding the Mercury to Salt and Sulphur.

Figures 8.4, 8.5 and 8.6-Completing the Conjunction.

Figure 8.7-The Alchemical Child within the Vessel.
Figure 8.8 and 8.9-Sealing the Vessel and the Sealed Embryo.

Figure 8.10 and 8.11-Labelling is VERY important, especially when doing more than a single tincture at a time.

Figure 8.12-Before a Maceration

Figure 8.13-After a Maceration

8.14-Protecting the Vessel and the Embryo from unwanted Light

Week 4-5 Alchemical Meditational Work

During your meditations during the week 4, you should continue to meditate on the breakdown of your herb, but this time within the solution of the menstruum. In your mind's eye, see the Mercury (or alcohol) breaking down the Salt (or herb). This is part of the phase of Nigredo for the herb, and as such see the Salts decomposing, putrefying, and becoming the very essence of the phase of Nigredo. Likewise, think about the purpose of your alchemical tincture. See the detriment that you are attempting to improve, or that part of yourself you wish to better or improve, being broken down in the same way within yourself. This is a 'softer' breaking up than in the previous week. Whereas last week you used a sledgehammer or tiller on the soil, this week, you would use a smaller hammer, to break the large bits into smaller bits, or if using the garden analogy, a rake to break up the soil rather than a tiller. It may help to visualize and place yourself inside the canister of your mixture and see the Mercury breaking down that part of yourself that you wish to improve. As you float within the fluid, visualize the Mercury eating away at that part of you that you wish to change. Each meditation should last between 5 and 20 minutes on these points.

For week 5, you will meditate specifically on the Sulphur (or oils) of the herb that have been now been drawn out by the Mercury. In your mind, see the Mercury (or alcohol) drawing out the Sulphur (or oil) of the herb. See that essence of Sulphur manifesting itself and becoming the new material of your mixture. Likewise, think about the purpose of your alchemical tincture. Continue to see yourself still immersed in the liquid solution. See the purpose and intent for what you are attempting to improve. As it manifests itself, and is drawn out of you by the Mercury, see these traits, or the Sulphur, having been drawn out the from the Salt of your being. Having been drawn out, it now floats within the Mercury as a single solution. Each meditation should last between 5 and 20 minutes on these points.

Week 4-5 Alchemical Homework

This week, after conceiving your alchemical child, you now need to macerate your herb for a few weeks. You should spend your time macerating your herb as a time to continue to connect with and energize your herb. Over the upcoming 2 weeks until the next section, you should perform 3 meditations per week relating to your herb, but remember to macerate (or shake it) twice per day.

Week 4-5 Summary

Congratulations! It's a Child!!! This week marks a very powerful one, in which you have created an energetic life form. You brought forth the Salt, or body, which was infused with the Sulphur, or the mind and unique nature of the herb, and you gave to it the Mercury, the Spirit, the very Breath of Life! This is a great accomplishment, but it should be remembered that you are still at the near beginnings of your alchemical work. Accomplishments are well deserved, but there is still much work ahead!

The upcoming weeks also mark a first, you will need to perform homework with your tincture mixture daily. At least once, and preferably two or three times per day, you should macerate, or shake, your solution, allowing it to draw as much of the Sulphur from the

Salts as possible. Being a responsible parent takes time and effort, but it will not be wasted. Caring for your new alchemical child is very important and will reap rewards and benefits down the road!

Week 4 Alchemical Journal - Entry 1

Name: _____ Date/Time: _____

Sun Sign: _____ Moon Sign: _____

Moon Phase: New / Waxing / Full / Waning / VoC

_____
_____
_____
_____
_____
_____
_____
_____
_____
_____
_____
_____
_____
_____
_____
_____
_____
_____
_____
_____
_____
_____
_____
_____
_____
_____
_____

Week 4 Alchemical Journal - Entry 2

Name: _____ Date/Time: _____

Sun Sign: _____ Moon Sign: _____

Moon Phase: New / Waxing / Full / Waning / VoC

_____

_____

_____

_____

_____

_____

_____

_____

_____

_____

_____

_____

_____

_____

_____

_____

_____

_____

_____

_____

_____

_____

_____

_____

_____

_____

Week 4 Alchemical Journal - Entry 3

Name: _____ Date/Time: _____

Sun Sign: _____ Moon Sign: _____

Moon Phase: New / Waxing / Full / Waning / VoC

_____
_____
_____
_____
_____
_____
_____
_____
_____
_____
_____
_____
_____
_____
_____
_____
_____
_____
_____
_____
_____
_____
_____
_____

Week 5 Alchemical Journal - Entry 1

Name: _____ Date/Time: _____

Sun Sign: _____ Moon Sign: _____

Moon Phase: New / Waxing / Full / Waning / VoC

_____

_____

_____

_____

_____

_____

_____

_____

_____

_____

_____

_____

_____

_____

_____

_____

_____

_____

_____

_____

_____

_____

_____

_____

Week 5 Alchemical Journal - Entry 2

Name: _____ Date/Time: _____

Sun Sign: _____ Moon Sign: _____

Moon Phase: New / Waxing / Full / Waning / VoC

_____

_____

_____

_____

_____

_____

_____

_____

_____

_____

_____

_____

_____

_____

_____

_____

_____

_____

_____

_____

_____

_____

_____

_____

_____

Week 5 Alchemical Journal - Entry 3

Name: _____ Date/Time: _____

Sun Sign: _____ Moon Sign: _____

Moon Phase: New / Waxing / Full / Waning / VoC

_____

_____

_____

_____

_____

_____

_____

_____

_____

_____

_____

_____

_____

_____

_____

_____

_____

_____

_____

_____

_____

_____

_____

_____

CHAPTER 6 – WEEK 6 SEPARATION OF THE ALCHEMICAL MIXTURE

Week 6 Procedures

This week, you will be performing the first Separation of your solution. Your herb has been macerated, and perhaps gone through, at least symbolically, the phases of putrefaction and fermentation, and now you will separate the original Salts of the herbal material, from the Mercury and Sulphur of the Menstruum solution, as the Sulphur of the herbal material is now found within the Menstruum as the oils from the herb.

Before beginning the process of Separation, you should once again bless, ordain or energize your herb (again, depending on whatever process your tradition may dictate, or just whatever feels right to you). Thank the Universe or deity for the process of change that has so far occurred, looking forward to what yet lies ahead. As you have continued to connect with your herb over the past few weeks, you should again, define your purpose, state it, say an invocation or blessing over it and send the energy and light of the divine into your material. This is a final consecration of the herb in its current state, before beginning to perform the separation.

Week 6 Alchemical Laboratory Work

The Separation of the Alchemical Mixture: Separating the Salts from the Mercury/Sulphur Menstruum

Now you will go through the process of separation. Perform the 'Entering the Alchemy Lab' meditation, and then bless, ordain or energize your herb with your purpose, according to your tradition, or using whatever method you would like. As you perform the filtration, you should be in a semi-meditative state. For this step you will need your two mason jars (one containing the menstruum and your herb and the other one empty) and the cheesecloth. Cut a piece of cheesecloth approximately 10 inches in length. Fold this in half, and lay it over the top of the empty mason jar. While holding the cheesecloth around the rim of the jar, gently press two fingers down into the center of the cheesecloth, creating a type of a funnel, going about 2-3 inches into the jar. While still holding the cheesecloth around the rim of the jar, slowly and carefully pour your alchemical mixture into the filter, allowing it to drain into the new jar. You may alternatively, use the ring of the mason jar lid and screw it on over the cheesecloth. While this may work, sometimes the weight of the herb will cause it to pull free, and you will need to continually remove and replace it to wring out the herb as the cheesecloth fills up. This is often more trouble than it's worth, but it is up to you. If you maintain a firm hold on the cheesecloth, you should be fine.

When the cheesecloth is relatively full, stop pouring and gently pull the filled cheesecloth out of the jar, bring the corners together to create a seal and twist it, to drain the maximum amount of Mercury and Sulphur from your mixture. Place the Salt of the herb from this process into your baking dish, and continue this process until all of the mixture has been separated in this way.

As you pour your mixture into the filtering mechanism, you should feel the Mercury, or the spirit of your material, being purified by the filtering process. Just as the liquid passes through the layers which trap and contain the material of the Salt of the herb, so too does your spirit pass through a filtering mechanism, purifying that part of yourself that you wish to improve or change. You will also be in very close contact with the Salt, Sulphur and Mercury of your herb. This presents a great opportunity to continue to connect with your herb and tune in your purpose with your herb.

As you perform this process, see the separation of the physical from the spiritual, both within your herb as well as within yourself. As you work with it, feel the separation taking place, smell it, experience it as you do your work.

Depending on how fine your herb has been ground, you may wish to repeat the filtering process a second or even several more times. You want to filter your mixture until there is only liquid remaining, with little or no trace of the herbal material. You will want to press or twist the herbal Salt, to extract as much of the Mercury as possible. You may also wish to use increasingly dense layers of cheesecloth in order to create a thicker and more tightly woven filter for the solution.

Sealing the Menstruum

At this point, we have two distinct parts of our material (remember, from our game analogy, currently your material is separated into two game pieces, the Sulphur/Mercury and the Salts); we have the physical herb, and the oil infused brandy. The oil infused brandy, which we term the Menstruum, contains the Sulphur, or identity of the herb, as well as well as the original Mercury, or Brandy. Some small amount of the Sulphur may be still contained within the Herb, or the Salts, or physical part of the herb. This is why we will continue to put the herb through a process of change, to continue to breakdown the Salts and extract the Sulphur. Then, we will perform a final Conjunction, called a Coagulation or recombination, of these substances to obtain our final Mercury solution, in the form of a completed tincture.

We are now done with the Menstruum or Mercury/Sulphur solution for a time. You will now seal your Mercury solution away in your jar for later use. Replace the wax paper with new and seal the jar. Place it at home in a location away from sunlight. You should perform a blessing or energize the Mercury and Sulphur solution a final time before putting it aside.

Distillation of the Salts

Now you will take your herbal salts (the leftover herbal material) and place them in your heat-resistant dish or glassware, and bake in your oven for between 1 and 2 hours at 200 degrees F. Stir occasionally with a glass or wooden rod or spoon until the herb is completely dry (the baking time will vary based on what herb you are working with). Allow to cool. Some ovens are gas-fired with an open flame. Using alcohol in such an environment is not recommended. Allow it to air-dry instead, by keeping your herb in a warm but dry location, where no wind or other activity can knock over or disturb the drying herbs. Make sure you stir it several times per day if you are air drying. The goal is not to transform the herb by the process of cooking it in the oven, but merely to completely dry it out for the upcoming calcination next week.

Figure 9.1-Revealing the developed Embryo.

Figure 9.2-The Saturation of the Mercury with the Sulphur.

Figure 9.3-Supplies needed for Separation and Filtration
Figure 9.4-Fashion a cheesecloth filtration funnel in the new vessel.

Figures 9.5, 9.6 and 9.7-Revealing the prepared embryo.

Figures 9.8 and 9.9-Viewing the Mercury and Sulphur from the top.

Figures 9.10, 9.11 and 9.12-Pouring the complete solution through the filtration mechanism.

Figures 9.13, 9.14 and 9.15-Rremove the filter from the vessel (be careful here, or the cheesecloth may fall back into the menstruum. If it does, re-pour the entire mixture back into the original vessel, rinse the new vessel, prepare a new piece of cheesecloth and begin to filter again).

Figure 9.16-The filtered Menstruum, containing the Sulphur and Mercury (after a single filtration).

Figures 9.17 and 9.18-The filtered Salts of the herb, still in the funnels. (Notice how they are twisted. You should twist or press the funnels to squeeze out the maximum amount of liquid that you can.)

Figures 9.19, 9.20- Performing a 2nd Filtration, with the cheesecloth doubled to filter out even more material.

Figures 9.21 and 9.22-Continuing the 2nd Filtration, with the cheesecloth doubled to filter out even more material.

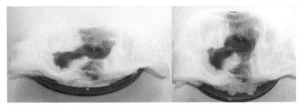

Figures 9.23 and 9.24-The filter from the 2nd filtration.

(Notice how it still captured a small amount of salts, but very little comparatively speaking.)

Figures 9.23-The filtered Menstruum Solution

Figures 9.24-The Menstruum, sealed in the vessel once again.

Figures 9.25-Placing the separated Salts into the Crucible/baking dish
Figures 9.26-Unwrapping the Salts.

Figures 9.27-The Salts before baking.
Figures 9.28-The Salts after baking for 30 minutes.

Figures 9.29- The Salts after baking for 60 minutes.
Figures 9.31- The Salts after baking for 90 minutes.

Figures 9.32- The Salts after baking for 120 minutes.
Figures 9.33-The dried Salts, prepared for the fires of Calcination.

Week 6 Alchemical Meditational Work

This week's meditation will very much mirror the physical process that you have just performed on your mixture. In your mind, see the process of separation that you performed. Relive the physical process of separation, of straining and purifying your herb. Smell the herb and the Menstruum, feel the liquid on your fingers and the sensation of the physical Salt of your herb, the unique smell of the Sulphur penetrating the air. Now, in your mind, envision that part of yourself that you wished to change and/or improve through this alchemical process. See that part of yourself separating from the larger and whole of 'you'. See it as a separate and distinct substance, just as the physical herb is separate and distinct from the Mercury and Sulphur Menstruum material. Now visualize yourself being poured and penetrating through several layers of cheesecloth, just as you did with your herb, and see the pure and changed 'you' straining out, and pouring into the jar as a purified substance, while the part of yourself you wish to change and leave behind is trapped within the layers of the filter. Recognize that this substance has been filtered out, and while still exists, is no longer a part of the pure 'you'. You should perform this meditation 3 times this week, and each meditation should last between 10 and 20 minutes. By this point, if you have been inexperienced at meditation, you should be able to lengthen your meditations by a bit. This is a very important part of the meditation, and it is highly encouraged that you begin to lengthen your meditations.

Week 6 Summary

This was a week to get your hands dirty! There is nothing so unique as the smell of a tincture at this phase. It is rich with the unique smell and essence of the herb, and represents that phase of Albedo. The smell, consistency and medicine of the finished tincture is all there. In fact, many tinctures you may purchase off the shelf at a health store are what you now have in your solution, the Mercury and the Sulphur of the herb. If you remember, some used to say that Albedo was the finished product, but we know that the change is not yet complete. We have Citrinitas and Rubedo yet to come. Smelling the tincture that some might consider completed, shows us that light at the end of the tunnel, or top of the well, but there is still work to be done to make this a true, alchemical tincture.

Week 6 Alchemical Journal - Entry 1

Name: _____ Date/Time: _____

Sun Sign: _____ Moon Sign: _____

Moon Phase: New / Waxing / Full / Waning / VoC

_____

_____

_____

_____

_____

_____

_____

_____

_____

_____

_____

_____

_____

_____

_____

_____

_____

_____

_____

_____

_____

_____

_____

_____

_____

Week 6 Alchemical Journal - Entry 2

Name: _____ Date/Time: _____

Sun Sign: _____ Moon Sign: _____

Moon Phase: New / Waxing / Full / Waning / VoC

_____

_____

_____

_____

_____

_____

_____

_____

_____

_____

_____

_____

_____

_____

_____

_____

_____

_____

_____

_____

_____

_____

_____

_____

_____

_____

_____

Week 6 Alchemical Journal - Entry 3

Name: _____ Date/Time: _____

Sun Sign: _____ Moon Sign: _____

Moon Phase: New / Waxing / Full / Waning / VoC

_____

_____

_____

_____

_____

_____

_____

_____

_____

_____

_____

_____

_____

_____

_____

_____

_____

_____

_____

_____

_____

_____

_____

_____

_____

_____

_____

_____

CHAPTER 7 – WEEK 7 CALCINATION OF THE SALTS

Week 7 Alchemical Procedures

This week, you will be performing the alchemical process of Calcination on your herb. The work in the previous week after separating the Salt, was to dry the herb Salts completely and have it in a state that will facilitate the transformation by Calcination. Now that the herb is dry we will apply an external heat to ignite the internal fire which will transform the base Salt of the herb, and will fundamentally change its chemical makeup to provide a purification by fire to the Salts.

As you have now dried your herb completely from the Menstruum solution, it is now ready to be prepared for the process of Calcination. As with all previous steps, before beginning, you should bless, ordain or energize your herb according to your tradition or using one of the general methods recommended previously. Bear in mind that you are now beginning to truly transform the Salt of your herb into a new and more pure substance, and thus you should ask for the blessings of the Divine for this purification and transformation. Also, before beginning the Calcination, and to better connect with your herb, you should smell and feel the Salt of your herb, taste it if you wish. This will enable you to experience the difference of your herb from its original state, to its current state, and a bit later, to compare the current state of the Salt, to its even more purified state.

Week 7 Alchemical Laboratory Work

For this process, your herb should be in a fire proof container, such as a stainless-steel bowl. Note that the bowl will become discolored and burned through the process, so you may want a dedicated bowl for this process rather than using your nice stainless mixing bowls! The goal during the Calcination process is to achieve the Whiteness of Albedo and begin to see the Redness of Rubedo, or the fires within. Ideally your herb should be a fine grey ash when completed. However practically, and without more sophisticated lab equipment, you will more than likely have a mixture of grey ash and blackened herb, which is fine. We will use specific methods later on in order to isolate the finer purified grey ash from the more impure blackened ash. Additionally, each herb burns differently, and while some will burn down almost completely, others need a bit more encouragement. Some of this blackened herb will filter out in the next process, so don't worry about getting the herb completely grey ash, although that is of course ideal.

There are a few different methods by which you can perform the Calcination. The first is the simplest and requires little to no equipment, however is also the most difficult to accomplish. For the first method, you may simply place your herb in its baking dish, on the uppermost rack in your oven, and bake it at the highest possible temperature, usually at a high broil. As mentioned, this is the simplest process, but it is very difficult to get very much, if any, grey ash in this process, and can also take a very long time.

If you have a hotplate, you may slowly burn your herb to ash over a hotplate. A hotplate can get VERY hot, and is the best method for the Calcination process. However, you must have a good hotplate, a proper crucible (a high temperature ceramic dish), and must watch over it very closely through the entire process.

Another method, and the one we will focus on in this workbook, is using a butane torch to burn the herb. Care should be taken, as a strong torch will cause the herb to blow and scatter. A Crème Brule style torch works excellent for this style of calcination as it is not too strong and will typically not blow the ash of the herb out of the bowl. You will want to apply the torch slowly, and try to get the herb to smolder. Smoldering will allow the herb to keep burning for a period of time, and will result in a better, more grey ash substance. Ideally, you should also ensure that you also use a Kevlar, or other heat resistant glove, to prevent your hand from getting burned while holding and working with the stainless-steel bowl.

The real goal is to get your herb to smolder slowly, not burn quickly. This is why a hotplate with a crucible is best, as you can regulate the temperature, and keep it smoldering at a steady rate. If you are using a butane torch as your flame source, hold the bowl steady, and burn 4 or 5 points of the herb. Hold the torch on each point for 10-15 seconds, then move on to the next one. After you have heated and started burning these 4 or 5 spots, shake the bowl gently to move the hot burning bits of herb to the bottom of the bowl, and repeat the process. Repeat that process 4 or 5 times over, and your herb should be at a point where it will burn and smolder on its own. It may still need some encouragement along the way if it starts to go out or cool down. The point is just do not hold the torch on it for 15 minutes, or it will all blacken. Allowing it to smolder is where the fine grey ash will come from.

As you perform this transformation, you should again be in a semi-meditative state, keeping the purpose of your alchemical experiment in mind. Once your herb is smoldering, you should again keep your herb within your sphere of sensation, or the area of your aura, and continue to connect with it. Smell it as it burns, as the smoke rises and the Salt of your herb transforms, feel it having that same transformative effect on you, burning away the impurities and transforming you (via the purpose of your herbal tincture) into something more pure; an altogether different material than before.

Once your herb has cooled sufficiently, you should reconnect to your herb by again touching, smelling and tasting it. Feel the difference in the Salt, how the physical material itself has changed in form into a new and different substance. Once you have connected to the new state of your material, you should once again energize, bless or ordain your herb to its purpose. As it is now a purer substance, and has been through the transformative fire, it is important to again give it its purpose and dedicate it to the divine.

Optional: If you are not happy with the state of your herb, it may be because the Salt of your herb is too coarse. We did not want to grind it too finely during week 3, as we did not want the Menstruum to become a 'muddy' substance. However, at this point, most herbs will smolder or burn more effectively and achieve a 'grey' state better if they are in a finer state. Use your mortar and pestle to grind your herb into a finer 'Salt', and then perform a second Calcination process on your herb. Be careful if it is windy, as the finer the material, the more it may be carried away by the wind.

Figure 10.1-The dried Salts, placed in the vessel
Figure 10.2-Begin by burning spots into the herb

Figure 10.3-Continue burning spots onto the herb
Figure 10.4-I like to burn a pattern like the 5 on a dice into the herb

Figure 10.5-After completing the spots, shake/circulate the herb to
move the smoldering herb to the bottom
Figure 10.6-Begin burning a similar pattern into the 'fresh' herb now
on top

Figure 10.7-Continue burning the spots in the herb
Figure 10.8-At a certain point, the spots will all merge, and much of the herb on top will be burning

Figure 10.9-Continuing to burn the herb
Figure 10.10-After another circulation, the overall herb is hot enough that much of it will tend to ignite

Figure 10.11-Continue shaking and burning until the herb is able to burn well enough on its own
Figure 10.12-Almost there, much of the herb is now burning and beginning to smolder

Figure 10.13-Now that nearly the entire herb has burned some and is igniting, it's time to let it sit and smolder to create the grey ash
Figure 10.14-The herb beginning to smolder

Figure 10.15-As long as it is smoking well, the herb is smoldering underneath
Figure 10.16-More grey ash beginning to appear

Figure 10.17-The grey areas are growing larger
Figure 10.18-The greying continues. If you enjoy divination, begin to notice patterns or shapes that you can interpret in the ash. Here, I see a small embryo appearing in the bottom left corner.

Figure 10.19-the smoldering has died down a bit
Figure 10.20-When it dies down, circulate the herb, as you did when burning it, but do not add more flame (yet). You will find that the influx of oxygen to new parts of the herb will rekindle the smoldering process.

Figure 10.21-Notice the heavier smoke again, indicating new and more smoldering
Figure 10.22-A new round of 'greying' begins

Figure 10.23-One more circulation of the ash
Figure 10.24-Another round of 'greying' begins

Figure 10.25-The more grey ash, the better
Figure 10.26-Again divining from the shape, notice the heart it is forming, or perhaps even two dragons facing one another.

Note: At this point, if the smoldering is dying down, you may need to apply the flame one more time to add some additional heat to continue the smoldering process. If you do, be careful, as the grey ash is very light, and you can lose a lot of it due to the 'wind' of the flame from the torch.

Once this process is completed, you should have enough grey ash to continue the process. However, for the purposes of demonstration, I will take the same ash and now burn it in a crucible at extremely high temperature to completely grey the entire herb. If you have this ability, it is certainly recommended, but it is not required. You will be separating the grey ash from the black in future processes, and will primarily use the grey ash.

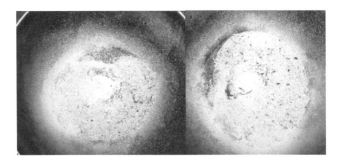

Figure 10.27-The herb after being in the crucible for about 6 minutes
Figure 10.28-The same, from a slightly different angle

Figure 10.29-The Herb in the crucible with the lights off
Figure 10.30-The completed Calcination from the Crucible. Note there is a much less quantity of ash remaining after burning in the crucible.

Figure 10.31-Prepare a vessel and funnel, in order to preserve as much of the ash as possible.
Figure 10.32-Place the ash into the vessel and seal it.

Week 7 Alchemical Meditational Work

Prior to this meditation, you need to come up with a mantra that fits the purpose of your transformation. For example, if I were trying to improve my physical health, I might say "I am a healthy person, I am part of the body of the Divine, and will keep my body a fit vessel for its Light". Spend a good amount of time, coming up with a mantra that fits the purpose of your alchemical child, fits with your tradition or belief system and is something you can easily remember.

As you meditate this week, remember back to the smoke of your Calcination process. Feel it around you, remember its smell and how it felt as your herb smoldered. Envision that part of yourself that you wish to change and/or improve through the alchemical process. Visualize the impure part of yourself, that which you wish to change, rising with the smoke and dissipating into nothingness. See also the Salt of your herb that you filtered in the last class, and see it changing, morphing into its new substance that you have created through the Calcination process. Then see that part of yourself that you are working on, and see it transform and change and improve. Recognize that this change is vital and important, yet is still only a portion of the overall change that is occurring and will continue to occur. See this change occurring in your daily life, envision yourself as if the changes were completed and you have achieved your end goal. As you end your meditation, repeat the mantra that you have created 3 times. You should also use your mantra throughout the week, when you wake, at mid-day, in the evening, and again before bed. You should perform this meditation 3 times this week, and each meditation should last between 10 and 20 minutes.

Week 7 Alchemical Homework

The practical homework this week is optional. If you wish to continue connecting with your herb, even after obtaining some degree of greying in your herb, you may continue to perform additional Calcinations on your herb in your oven, crucible or with a torch. As it undergoes the Calcination process, continue to connect with your herb and feel the transformation both in your herb, as well as in yourself.

Week 7 Summary

Burn, baby burn! This week was one of great transformation! The element of fire can cause great devastation, but it also prepares the way for the subtler changes and influences of Water. Once again, Fire is the motorized tiller, to the Rake of Water. Your herb at this point, should be essentially unrecognizable. It has changed to where it does not look, feel nor taste the same, yet we know that it still is the same substance with which you started, merely transformed into something new. This is the same with you. Your transformation should be entering a phase where you may not recognize certain parts or traits about yourself. You are beginning to recognize that you do not like certain parts of yourself, and that is why you have taken on the challenge to change. Once you have reached this point, there is no going back. You cannot turn the ash back into an herb, and you cannot return yourself back to the state which you were in previously. Time to forge ahead, and continue your path of improvement and enlightenment!

Week 7 Mantra

Use the spaces below to work on and write out the Mantra that you will use this week:

_____

_____

_____

_____

_____

_____

_____

_____

_____

_____

_____

_____

<u>Final Mantra:</u>

_____

_____

_____

_____

_____

Week 7 Alchemical Journal - Entry 1

Name: _____ Date/Time: _____

Sun Sign: _____ Moon Sign: _____

Moon Phase: New / Waxing / Full / Waning / VoC

_____

_____

_____

_____

_____

_____

_____

_____

_____

_____

_____

_____

_____

_____

_____

_____

_____

_____

_____

_____

_____

_____

_____

Week 7 Alchemical Journal - Entry 2

Name: _____ Date/Time: _____

Sun Sign: _____ Moon Sign: _____

Moon Phase: New / Waxing / Full / Waning / VoC

_____
_____
_____
_____
_____
_____
_____
_____
_____
_____
_____
_____
_____
_____
_____
_____
_____
_____
_____
_____
_____
_____
_____
_____

Week 7 Alchemical Journal - Entry 3

Name: _____ Date/Time: _____

Sun Sign: _____ Moon Sign: _____

Moon Phase: New / Waxing / Full / Waning / VoC

_____

_____

_____

_____

_____

_____

_____

_____

_____

_____

_____

_____

_____

_____

_____

_____

_____

_____

_____

_____

_____

_____

_____

_____

CHAPTER 8
WEEK 8 – DISSOLUTION OF THE SALTS

Week 8 Alchemical Procedures

This week, you will be enacting the process of dissolution on your Salts. Last week, you performed a Calcination, and fundamentally changed the physical appearance, or Salt of your herb. This represents a transformation by fire of the Salt of the herb, and we will now extract those Salts that have been purified by fire, for use in your final tincture, when we will bring back together the Salt, Sulphur and Mercury of your herb.

Fire is the great destroyer, and Water is the giver of life. Last week, we broke down the Salts and completely transformed them through the violence and destructive nature of Fire. This week, you will dissolve the ash into the Water, again to transform it but this time with the gentle nature of water, giving life back to that which was dead and burned.

After separating the ash, and getting only the most fine, pure and fit ash for alchemical work, you will place that ash into water and watch it dissolve into the water, yet another transformation from the seen into the unseen world. This causes another chemical change, which will again purify and fundamentally change the structure and substance of your Salts.

Week 8 Alchemical Laboratory Work

First, as before, you should perform the 'Entering the Alchemy Lab' meditation and bless the Calcinated Salt of your herb according to your tradition. Next, you will use a simple kitchen sieve to separate the purer ash of your calcinated herb, from the larger pieces that did not burn completely. This is the second separation that you have performed on your herb. The first was the separation of the Salt from the Sulphur and Mercury of your herb. Now, we are separating the 'Wheat' from the 'Chaff', obtaining only the Salts that were the most purified by the fires of Calcination.

If you like, you may take the larger pieces of ash that would not filter through the sieve, and regrind them in a mortar and pestle. After that, you would put it through the calcination process and then pass it through the sieve again. If you choose not to repeat that process, you may dispose of it by giving it back to the earth, using it as incense or any other good purpose that you may have for it. Remember that you have given a significant amount of time and energy to all of the Salts at this time, and discarding in the trash or down a sink would be a waste of that energy. A good way to discard of it is to return it to nature, thus giving your time and energy back to that which gave it (and you) life.

Now that you have separated your purified Salts, or ash, we will be purifying them with water. The amount of water used can vary widely. Some sources say that you should add approximately 6-8 times the volume of distilled water as the ash. Others say a set amount of water for each ounce of herb, for example 1 ounce of water for each 1 ounce of herb that you began the process with. In the end, you must judge if you have enough water to dissolve most the ashes. This is a place where the best judge is you, who can observe the outcome of the Conjunction.

You should add enough water so that the ash is dissolved, and there is no visible ash floating 'within' the water. There will always be a few pieces that do not dissolve, and they typically will float on top of the water. Don't worry these will be filtered out in the next steps, just make sure that the finer ash is completely dissolved.

As you perform the Conjunction of the water and the Salts, you should do so in a meditative state, seeing the purity of the Salt of the herb, combining with the purity of the distilled water. You also don't want to use too much water, or the evaporating step will take much longer.

Seal your jar in preparation for next week, and use the solution of the dissolution as your meditative focus for the remainder of this week.

Figure 11.1-The calcinated ash in the vessel
Figure 11.2-You will need the ash, a kitchen sieve, an empty vessel and distilled water

Figure 11.3-Place the kitchen sieve over the empty vessel.

Figure 11.4-Begin pouring the ash into the sieve. Shake it gently (you don't want your ash to go outside of the vessel, so you'll want to add small amounts at a time).

Figure 11.5-Finish placing all of the ash through the sieve/filter.

Figure 11.6-See the following Note.

Note: When completed, you will likely have some larger bits of ash in the sieve. You have several options. You may take it and sacrifice it back to nature. Either burn it as incense, or give it back to the Earth. You may also use your thumb or finger, as in Figure 11.6 to gently press some of the ash through the filter, causing it to break apart into smaller pieces. You may also choose to re-Calcinate the leftover pieces and see if they breakdown into a finer and more purified ash.

Figure 11.7, 11.8 and 11.9-Slowly add the distilled water to the calcinated ash

Figure 11.10-Continue adding water until a the grey ash has dissolved
Figure 11.11-Stop at various intervals to see if you need more water

Figure 11.12-You will notice some blackened ash that did not dissolve, and
that is fine. However, you want the grey ash to be completely dissolved.
Figure 11.13-A view f the same from the top.

Figure 11.14-A close up view of the cloudy mixture, with some blackened
ash.
Figure 11.15-Seal the vessel until next week.

Week 8 Alchemical Meditational Work

As you have now Calcinated your herb, and purified it by fire, you will next be cleansing and purifying it by water. For your meditation this week, you should see you and that aspect of yourself that you wish to change, as a completely purified substance. The changes that you wish to make have now dissolved into your subconscious mind, just as the ash has dissolved into the distilled water. These changes are now beginning to permeate into your very being, becoming a part of who you are. You have progressed a long way, and now you are in a changed state, ready for the light of the divine to take residence. Now, see that final purification by water, that you have taken your purified state and immersed it into pure water, causing the new you to dissolve into the purified water, only to begin to now crystalize and form into a stronger form and a stronger virtue. See this new substance as the most pure, holy and divine substance in the universe. See this substance of the Salt of your herb, and yourself, as one and the same. You should perform this meditation a minimum of three times, and each meditation should last 10-20 minutes.

Week 8 Alchemical Homework

There is not homework this week except for performing the mediation at least 3 times, for a duration of 10-25 minutes each.

Week 8 Summary

Come on in, the Water's fine! Just as last week marked a definite point of no return, this week also marks a turning point in your journey. When developing a new part of yourself, whether breaking an old habit, developing a new one, or changing some aspect of yourself, there comes a time when that 'new' part of yourself, starts to become second nature. It has 'dissolved' into your subconscious mind, and no longer requires conscious thought to perform or act. This is the process of dissolution. You have taken the purified ash from the fires, and dissolved them into the Living Waters, there to be assimilated and made part of the greater whole. This is an exciting time, and the light at the end of the tunnel (or the top of the well) is getting closer and brighter!

Week 8 Alchemical Journal - Entry 1

Name: _____ Date/Time: _____

Sun Sign: _____ Moon Sign: _____

Moon Phase: New / Waxing / Full / Waning / VoC

_____

_____

_____

_____

_____

_____

_____

_____

_____

_____

_____

_____

_____

_____

_____

_____

_____

_____

_____

_____

_____

_____

_____

_____

_____

_____

_____

_____

Week 8 Alchemical Journal - Entry 2

Name: _____ Date/Time: _____

Sun Sign: _____ Moon Sign: _____

Moon Phase: New / Waxing / Full / Waning / VoC

_____

_____

_____

_____

_____

_____

_____

_____

_____

_____

_____

_____

_____

_____

_____

_____

_____

_____

_____

_____

_____

_____

_____

Week 8 Alchemical Journal - Entry 3

Name: _____ Date/Time: _____

Sun Sign: _____ Moon Sign: _____

Moon Phase: New / Waxing / Full / Waning / VoC

_____

_____

_____

_____

_____

_____

_____

_____

_____

_____

_____

_____

_____

_____

_____

_____

_____

_____

_____

_____

_____

_____

_____

_____

_____

CHAPTER 9
WEEK 9 – PURIFICATION BY FILTRATION

Week 9 Alchemical Procedures

This week, you will be filtering out the changed body of the Salt of your herb, in preparation for the Distillation and final Coagulation with the Menstruum, or the Sulphur and Mercury solution.

The filtrations serve to filter out the impurities from the solution. In life, these are the checks that we give ourselves. For example, if you were attempting to break a bad habit, you might remove from around yourself things that remind you of that habit, or that cause you to participate in it. Leaving remnants around only serve to tempt you to fall back into old patterns. Filtration serves the same purpose, by eliminating the impurities from the substance, which may weaken its overall potency and effects.

Week 9 Alchemical Laboratory Work

To filter the liquid solution, you will pour your Salt solution into another container through a cheesecloth funnel, as you did in the first filtration of the menstruum. You may perform this process as many times as you like. As with the previous separation process, you should see and feel this final separation of the salt, and as your Salt becomes more and more pure in its essence, so should you feel that change within yourself, seeing that part of yourself that you are working on, becoming more and more pure, with each filtration. The goal is to only retain the purest form of the Salt in your solution as possible. Your water does not need to be completely clear, but should not have any larger pieces of ash or the visible salts floating in the mixture. This will certainly vary somewhat depending upon your herb, and its coloring and consistency after the Calcination process. You should also use increasingly dense layers of cheesecloth as you filter, to draw out the most impure of the Salts. You should filter it at least 3 times, although you may wish to do it more often.

Figure 12.1-You need the dissolved ash, another vessel and cheesecloth.
Figure 12.2-Create a funnel, as you did when doing the first separation.

Figure 12.3, 12.4 and 12.5-Pour the mixture through the cheesecloth in order to separate the pure from the impure, the wheat from the chaff, the worthy from the unworthy.

Figure 12.6 and 12.7-Notice as you get to the bottom, the darker ash will be caught in the separatory filter.

Figure 12.8-You will likely have some sludge and ash remaining in the bottom of the vessel. You may either discard this, or if you wish, add a few tablespoons of distilled water to allow it to reabsorb, and then run it through the separatory filter as well.

Figure 12.9-The filter after the first filtration.
Figure 12.10-The filter after the second filtration.

Note: You may do as many filtrations as you wish. I typically perform 3, but you may choose 3, 7, 9, 12 or any mystical number which may have significance for you.

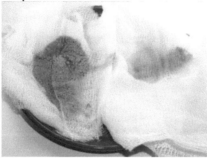

Figure 12.11-A side by side comparison of the first and second filters.

Figure 12.12-Seal the filtered solution until next week.

Figures 12.13 and 12.14-A side by side comparison of before and after the separartion by filtration process.

Week 9 Alchemical Meditational Work

You will now be preparing for the final Coagulation of your herb. You should view your purified body, purified soul and purified spirit, each one representing the three alchemical principles of Salt, Sulphur and Mercury. See them becoming united, not only changing or improving the area that you have chosen, but far exceeding even your own expectations. See these three principles that you have worked with reuniting, even as they symbolically reunite within yourself. As they reunite, see deep within yourself a glowing white radiance, continuing to grow larger and larger, until it fills your entire being, and the entirety of your aura. Then imagine it continuing to grow, expanding to fill the room you are in, the house in which you reside, until that light has grown so vast, it fills even the vastness of space. Slowly, come back to yourself, recognize the feeling of the ground under your feet, your surroundings, but continue to be aware of that white light deep within yourself. Consider that each time you partake of your completed tincture, you will be going through the exact process just described in this mediation. You should perform this meditation 3 times, and each one should be between 15-25 minutes.

Week 9 Alchemical Homework

This week's alchemical work is one of separation, separating the wheat from the chaff, the pure from the impure. This is a critical separation before the final recombination of the two substances into a final whole.

Week 9 Summary

There is a lesson in purification this week that is profound. Often the purest is also the least dense or least in overall quantity. If you look at the amount of Salts that you have left, compared with what you started with, it is probably a thimble full compared to a bowl full. Yet, this thimble full of Salt contains the purified energy of thousands of times its volume or weight that the original Salt held. It is truly amazing and humbling, and should reveal to you some of the most true and profound secrets in alchemy and magic.

Week 9 Alchemical Journal - Entry 1

Name: _____ Date/Time: _____

Sun Sign: _____ Moon Sign: _____

Moon Phase: New / Waxing / Full / Waning / VoC

_____
_____
_____
_____
_____
_____
_____
_____
_____
_____
_____
_____
_____
_____
_____
_____
_____
_____
_____
_____
_____
_____

Week 9 Alchemical Journal - Entry 2

Name: _____ Date/Time: _____

Sun Sign: _____ Moon Sign: _____

Moon Phase: New / Waxing / Full / Waning / VoC

_____

_____

_____

_____

_____

_____

_____

_____

_____

_____

_____

_____

_____

_____

_____

_____

_____

_____

_____

_____

_____

_____

_____

_____

_____

Week 9 Alchemical Journal - Entry 3

Name: _____ Date/Time: _____

Sun Sign: _____ Moon Sign: _____

Moon Phase: New / Waxing / Full / Waning / VoC

CHAPTER 10 – WEEK 10 PURIFICATION BY DISTILLATION AND THE COAGULATION OF THE SALT, SULPHUR AND MERCURY

Week 10 Alchemical Procedures

This week, you will be performing the Distillation and final Coagulation of your alchemical mixture, combining the Menstruum, containing the Sulphur and Mercury, with the Salts that you have transformed through fire, water and your own energy. At this point, you have extracted the Sulphur from your herb, using a Mercurial substance, thus giving you your liquid Menstruum. In addition, you have taken the original Salt of your herb, and put it through several transformative processes: Separation, Calcination, Filtration, Dissolution and now Distillation. When completed, you will have a very different, and much purer 'Salt' substance, which vibrates at a much higher level due to both the purifications and the energy which you have provided to it. Throughout the entire process, you have blessed, ordained, consecrated or energized your 3 alchemical substances multiple times, with your intent. This, in and of itself, has a transformative effect on the materium (as well as upon yourself). Notice how different your material looks than what you started with for this process. It should be a significant change; in fact, your Salts should be unrecognizable from what you started with.

You will perform a type of distillation on the Salt solution, by baking and evaporating the water from the solution. This will yield the final Salts, which will be added to the Sulphur/Mercury solution to create your final alchemical Tincture. These Salts have been purified by the Immortal Fire, immersed in the Living Waters and then Distilled to create a new concentrated and very potent substance. When this new substance is added to the menstruum solution, it will then yield a method by which the alchemical Tincture can manifest its benefits into existence within you.

Week 10 Alchemical Laboratory Work
Distillation of your Salt solution

Take your Salt Solution from the previous week and pour it into your baking tray, or crucible. You want to bake it at about 200 degrees until the water is evaporated and you have a crystallization of the salts in the bottom of your dish. You do not want to bring the water to a boil, as that can have an unwanted transformative effect on the Salt, which is why we keep it below 200 degrees.

After the water has completely evaporated, you will be left with a small layer of the final Salts on the bottom of your baking dish. They will often have a greasy appearance to them after transforming. Use a Razor blade to scrape the Salts off the bottom of your baking dish, and place them carefully into a vessel or container. These are the Holy Salts, which have been cleansed and transformed by fire, and purified and transformed by water. You will no doubt notice that you probably have much less material left in the end, after the calcination, filtration, dissolution and distillation processes. These are only the purest Salts, and have an extremely high vibration due to the processes they have been through, and the energy that you have given them throughout this process.

Coagulation of your Alchemical Tincture

Now, you will take these Salts from your herb, and once again, bless or energize it with your purpose. At this point, you may wish to take a small pinch (likely a very small pinch), and give it as a sacrifice back to the Universe. You may place it into the earth, release it into the winds, allow it to dissolve into water, or burn it along with some appropriate incense as a burnt sacrifice. This shows the universe, your deity or deities, that after working so hard on the Salt of your herb, you are willing to give some small part of it back to the source.

Next, take the Sulphur and Mercury solution, and once again, bless or energize it with your purpose. You may want to take a few drops of this solution and sacrifice it in a similar method to the Salts. In a meditative state, Coagulate, or combine, the transformed Salts with the original Menstruum of Sulphur and Mercury. This is not an exact process, and depending on the amount of materials that you have, you may want to use more or less of your Salts. You DO NOT want your final mixture to be cloudy or gritty with the Salt, so do not simply pour all the Salts into the solution. It is advisable to add a small amount of the Salt to the Sulphur and Mercury, stir it in, evaluate, and continue adding until you are satisfied with your mixture.

As you Coagulate your materium, consider that this is the final alchemical process you are performing, and whereas you created or conceived of your alchemical child in the Second Class, you are now witnessing it becoming its full potential. This is the true birth of your alchemical child. This is a sacred time, and a sacred operation, and just as you are creating and witnessing the flowering of a sacred spiritual substance, so too are you yourself, becoming the same sacred and spiritual being, flowering into your full potential and becoming a permanent vessel for the light of the Divine.

Consecration of your Alchemical Tincture

Lastly, you should perform a final Consecration on your Tincture. This should be very powerful, very energetic and in fact you should likely prefer to perform your final consecration in the confines of your own temple or magical/alchemical working area where you can focus more and utilize the tools of your tradition, or even plan a complete ritual around it, that would be very appropriate.

Once you have completed the Coagulation, you may either keep your tincture material in your jar, or you may transfer a small amount into a smaller, decorative container for direct use.

Consumption of your Alchemical Tincture

Directions for ingesting your tincture vary. You may take anywhere from 2-20 drops of your tincture with a cup of water. You may wish to start off with 2-3 drops, and increase gradually. Alternatively, you may place 2-10 drops directly under your tongue for faster absorption, and to avoid the digestive process of the stomach. When I am using a tincture to prepare for a magical event, I start 2-3 weeks' prior with 2-3 drops, and gradually increase the dosage. For the final 2-3 days before, I use it directly under the tongue for the greatest benefit, as well as taking it with water. That way I get the immediate absorption into the bloodstream as well as the prolonged effect via the digestive system.

You may also choose to use it in conjunction with the timing of an element (as per the Zodiacal signs), a planet (as per the planetary days and hours) or other meaningful time relating to your path or tradition.

Remember that every herb is different, and this is why I advise to begin small, and gradually increase the dosage, to ensure that you do not have an adverse effect to an immediate large dosage. From this point on, it is not necessary to ever re-consecrate or energize your tincture. It has been through the alchemical process, and has taken on a life of its own. You energized and nurtured it along its way, and it has now matured into the Summum Bonum, that final stage, and in fact to consider re-energizing it now, would show a lack of faith on your part, and could spiritually deconstruct what you have made.

Week 10 Alchemical Meditation Work

Anytime you feel that you need to do so, perhaps to reinforce the work that you did over the course of creating this tincture, you can meditate with your tincture material and even use the mantra that you created during week 7. As before, see the aura of the tincture (this should be much easier now, as it has much of your essence infused into it); see the ribbon of energy connecting it to your own aura, and tune your frequency to the same color, strength and vibration. Communicate with the tincture and herb, remember your purpose, ask for its help and strength in accomplishing your own Great Work.

Week 10 Homework

The only homework after this class is to perform your final consecration in your own private area if you wish, and to partake of your tincture for a good length of time, to allow it to work on your purpose that you gave it. Remember that the work on the tincture itself is completed, however its work on you, your body, spirit and soul, is not.

Week 10 Summary

Congratulations! It's been a long road of 2 ½ months or longer at this point, but you've stuck with it and created your very first spagyric, or alchemical Tincture. It is not an easy process, but one that yields amazing benefits of body, mind and spirit. Remember that each time you ingest the tincture that you have made, you are partaking of the energy that you imbued, grew and purified into the original herb, as well as the energy of that herb returning to you. It is a very potent medicine and can affect you not only in visible, but also in unseen ways. Keep up the good work, there are not only hundreds of herbs which you can work and grow with, but other alchemical methods to continue your own alchemical work and path!

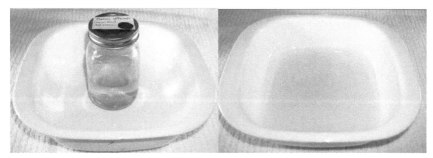

Figure 13.1-The dissolved Salts and the Crucible
Figure 13.2-Pour the contents into the crucible

Figure 13.3-After baking for 20 minutes
Figure 13.4- After baking for 40 minutes

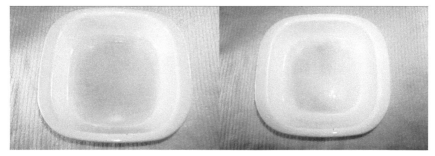

Figure 13.5- After baking for 60 minutes
Figure 13.6- After baking for 80 minutes

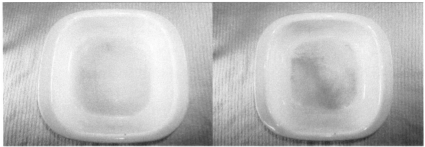

Figure 13.7- After baking for 100 minutes
Figure 13.8- After baking for 120 minutes

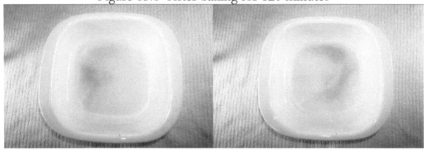

Figure 13.9- After baking for 140 minutes
Figure 13.10- After baking for 160 minutes

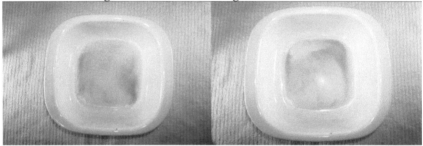

Figure 13.11- After baking for 180 minutes
Figure 13.12- After baking for 200 minutes

Figure 13.13- After baking for 220 minutes
Figure 13.14- After baking for 240 minutes

Figure 13.15- Completed after approximately 4 hours
Figure 13.16- Use a razor blade to scrape the Salts from the bottom
of the crucible

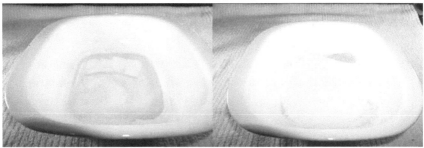

Figure 13.17- While the Salts are sometimes difficult to see, once you
begin scraping you can see the difference
Figure 13.18- All of the Salts scraped, ready to be reintegrated with
the Sulphur/Mercury solution

Figure 13.19-To complete the Coagulation, you will need the purified
Salts and the Menstruum solution, consisting of the Sulphur and
Mercury
Figure 13.20- Remove the seal from the Menstruum and the Salts

Figure 13.21- Begin adding the Salts to the Menstruum solution. This is the moment of birth.

Figure 13.22- Continue adding the Salts

Figure 13.23- Stir the mixture. You want to dissolve the salts to the point of saturation, so when you can see the Salts in the mixture, stop. However, it may easily absorb all of the Salts as well.

Figure 13.24- The Alchemical Child within the Vessel

Figure 13.25- Performing a final Maceration on the solution can ensure that all of the Salts are fully integrated

Figure 13.26- The Completed Alchemical Child
Figure 13.27-Although optional, you may wish to decorate a smaller
'dosing' bottle to carry with you. This one was for a tincture of
Sol/Fire, so the symbols are different, but the image is an example of
how you might decorate the bottle so that it speaks to you each time
you use it.

Week 10 Alchemical Journal - Final Coagulation

Name: _____ Date/Time: _____

Sun Sign: _____ Moon Sign: _____

Moon Phase: New / Waxing / Full / Waning / VoC

_____

_____

_____

_____

_____

_____

_____

_____

_____

_____

_____

_____

_____

_____

_____

_____

_____

_____

_____

_____

_____

_____

_____

_____

_____

_____

_____

Week 10 Alchemical Journal - Consecration Ritual Journal Entry

Name: _____ Date/Time: _____

Sun Sign: _____ Moon Sign: _____

Moon Phase: New / Waxing / Full / Waning / VoC

_____

_____

_____

_____

_____

_____

_____

_____

_____

_____

_____

_____

_____

_____

_____

_____

_____

_____

_____

_____

_____

_____

CHAPTER 11
WORKBOOK WRAP-UP

Congratulations! As you continue to ingest and work with your tincture over the upcoming days, weeks, months and potentially years, you will see the benefits and change that occurs when working with a particular herb, plant, flower or tree. As has been stated previously, there are literally thousands of herbs, plants, flowers and trees on this planet. Now that you've completed a tincture of one of them, you can see the huge world of plant spirits waiting to invest you with their wisdom! Truly, a lifetime of learning!

As you proceed on your path as an Alchemist, if, in your experimenting, you run into stumbling blocks (and you will), remember what Paracelsus had his students write over their labs:

PATIENCE!

Nothing in this work comes fast, but it is all of great value in the end. Also, never forget that even though we are discussing how to perform chemical operations, ultimately they all apply, as do the rituals, to internal aspects of yourself. Always meditate on how your stages, processes and elements relates to your own personal transmutation.

Alchemical Initiations

I am personally a believer in initiation as a gateway to enlightenment. Just as it would be nearly impossible to teach yourself how to build a computer from scratch (including the processor, memory, circuit boards, etc.), so too is it nearly impossible for us to completely attain the empyrean heights of human consciousness without a guide of some sort. And just as we might graduate from High School, College and Graduate school to gain the education needed in order to build a computer from nothing, so we need initiation (to go along with the teachings) to open us up to the energies and experiences that await you, should you choose to continue your journey.

In today's world of the Internet, where nearly anything can be found merely by typing it into a search engine, many think that the ideas of initiation, training and accomplishment with a qualified mentor is at an end. I personally do not believe that to be the case. If you do, that's fine, we can agree to disagree, and that's fine, we are allowed to do so. It is my opinion, in working over 30 years with various spiritual systems, that initiation and instruction are amazing aides in advancing your own spiritual learning and progression.

I personally view initiation as a 3-fold and 3-part process. It is 3-fold in that a true initiation has an effect upon the body, mind and spirit of the initiate. In learning online, or undergoing a 'self-initiations', the physical aspect of surprise and/or shock is often missing. This is one of the aspects that is often overlooked in online correspondence courses or other remote/distance learning situations.

It is a 3-part process as many ancient schools have 3 degrees (or at least 3 major ones) which are passed through during the initiatory process. It may be called beginner, intermediate, advanced; novice, journeyman, advanced; neophyte, initiate, adept, or many other titles that may be used to describe these levels. However numerous mystery schools follow this same rule of three. If initiation is of interest to you, you have a few options.

You can learn from books, online resources or other correspondence courses that are available and work towards a type of self-initiation. I myself offer remote learning opportunities for students of many levels. These can be great, I have done many of them myself, and there is definitely a great amount of learning that can be done this way. They can also be very lacking, and quite simply money machines for those running them. You can follow this path and even become an expert in the field, though it will likely take a while.

You could also try to find a qualified teacher, learn from them and follow the path that they lay out for you (which may or may not include what I refer to as 'initiations'). Individual teachers have a lot to offer and will often give you dedicated instruction time. You may even have a combination of online classes and learning coupled with occasional in-person classes, training and initiations, which is also what I do with many of my students, both local and remote.

Either way that you go, you will learn things about alchemy, about magic, about the Universe and about yourself that you would have never thought possible. Building a computer from scratch is a very complicated and detailed process, but imagine your elation if you completed such a task on your own! Now, imagine that you had someone who already knew HOW to build a computer, had the knowledge that they could pass on to you. Think about how accelerated that process would be, with a knowing mentor at your side, pointing out possible errors, shortcuts or more efficient ways of doing things. There is still an element of self-discovery, of learning to customize the path to oneself after learning from someone else, however this greatly accelerates the process of learning, growth and enlightenment. Coupled with initiation, which does the same for the spirit (i.e. it opens it up to new energies, thoughts and processes, enables quicker learning and assimilation of spiritual knowledge), I believe that learning with a teacher or group/organization is a much more efficient process.

If you are truly interested in working with a teacher or mentor, then do so! Find one that seems to teach the way that caters to your learning style. Understand that you may need to do some travelling to do so, but that it is worth it many times over. I am also working on a book of initiations for the solo alchemist that will cover many secrets of alchemy, put into a ritual initiatory process, that will give you some of the benefits of opening up your spirit to new energies.

If that is of interest to you, consider this book a first step on that path. It begins to orient your spirit, your mind, your body and nature to the path of alchemy. While basic in its process, if followed and used as intended, the spiritual implications and progress that you can make can be immense! These initiations will then assist you in moving along that path of initiation, and the whole of the entire process, leading you at length to the attainment of the Quintessence, the Stone of the Wise, true wisdom and perfect happiness, the Summum Bonum.

ABOUT THE AUTHOR

Frater M.T.O. has been a student of the spiritual mysteries for most of his life, including being a practicing Alchemist, Magician and Occultist for over 20 years. He teaches classes on Alchemy and Magic the Denver Colorado area and has taught hundreds of students over the past 10 years. He has studied within several schools of alchemy, is a member of the International Alchemy Guild, and has completed guild's Alchemy Study Program as well as having completed the Philosophers of Nature coursework. He is the Chief Adept of the Order of the Golden Dawn in the Outer headquartered in Denver, CO. He has been a featured speaker on numerous blogs and radio shows regarding Alchemy including VH Frater BT's "The Esoterinerd Podcast" and the "Dr. Mike After Dark" radio show.

His alchemy blog, Alembic Alchemy, has thousands of subscribers and he has recently launched an online alchemy academy for those interested in learning more about Alchemy. Both the blog and academy of classes have been recently combined into a single website with his metaphysical store, Ye Olde Magic Shoppe (www.yeoldemagicshoppe.com), which he owns with his partner. He currently resides in Denver Colorado with his wonderful family and amazing partner, Soror MIMM.

CPSIA information can be obtained
at www.ICGtesting.com
Printed in the USA
LVHW070958180222
711467LV00010B/26